God's gift will be evident in the pages of this book. Mike easily identifies for his reader their present spiritual location and he gives a clear biblical road map to God's desired destination. In this book, you will find powerful and insightful direction for your life.

-Pastor Robert Faulk, House of Mercy Ministries

I met Michael approximately twenty-five years ago when he was without God and without hope. Seeing Michael today is a complete contrast from his former self and now I see it written on the pages of this amazing book. The insight Michael has concerning souls is amazing and on target for past, present, and future readers. Let the words of this book be a path to lead you to the One who created you.

-Pastor Jeff Casey

Mike is motivated to see the believer experience God's best in their life. His book sheds light on our blind spots, as knowing the truth can truly set us free!

-Pastor/Elder Randy Dyer, Hope Christian Community Church

Not only has Mike lived this himself, but the simple truths that he is sharing will help to transform your life.

-Pastor Raynard Sands, Be Like Jesus Ministries

Putting Away Childish Things

Putting Away Childish Things

PACT

KEYS TO UNLOCKING YOUR GOD-GIVEN POTENTIAL

Michael P. Lovrick

XULON PRESS

Xulon Press
2301 Lucien Way #415
Maitland, FL 32751
407.339.4217
www.xulonpress.com

© 2022 by Michael P. Lovrick

All rights reserved solely by the author. The author guarantees all contents are original and do not infringe upon the legal rights of any other person or work. No part of this book may be reproduced in any form without the permission of the author.

Due to the changing nature of the Internet, if there are any web addresses, links, or URLs included in this manuscript, these may have been altered and may no longer be accessible. The views and opinions shared in this book belong solely to the author and do not necessarily reflect those of the publisher. The publisher therefore disclaims responsibility for the views or opinions expressed within the work.

Unless otherwise indicated, Scripture quotations taken from the King James Version (KJV) – *public domain;* The New American Standard Bible (NASB). Copyright © 1960, 1962, 1963, 1968, 1971, 1972, 1973, 1975, 1977, 1995 by The Lockman Foundation. Used by permission. All rights reserved; the New International Version (NIV). Copyright © 1973, 1978, 1984, 2011 by Biblica, Inc.™. Used by permission. All rights reserved; the English Standard Version (ESV). Copyright © 2001 by Crossway, a publishing ministry of Good News Publishers. Used by permission. All rights reserved; The New King James Version (NKJV). Copyright © 1982 by Thomas Nelson, Inc. Used by permission. All rights reserved;

Paperback ISBN-13: 978-1-66282-849-2
Ebook ISBN-13: 978-1-66283-295-6

DEDICATION

To my amazing sons Philip and Cory, my incredible daughter-in-law Shannon, and my precious granddaughter Leila. Their unconditional love, support, and unwavering belief in me are the inspiration behind me taking this leap of faith so late in life.

To Pastors Bob Faulk, Randy Dyer, Raynard Sands, and Jeffery Casey, as well as Chaplain Joshua Sendawula and Chaplain Zilvanis Jakstas for believing in me and seeing in me the God-given potential that I never saw in myself.

To Becci and Dave Householder, for their love, support, and encouragement thru some challenging times.

To James Barker for his Christ-like love and friendship, and for always telling me that my emails were more like e-novels.

To Andrew Raymond for all the laps we walked around the track talking about a time such as this.

To DeAnn Nesbitt for her patience and professionalism in painstakingly editing my book to make sure it was perfect.

To all my brothers in chains for encouraging me, holding me accountable, and for constantly reminding me that ALL things are possible through Christ.

To Glenn from House of Mercy, for patiently walking me through all the technical stuff and answering all my questions regarding how to get this book formatted for publishing.

And lastly special thanks to Jennifer Smith, for her tireless support, undeniable compassion, and unbelievable encouragement in standing by me when I needed it the most.

CONTENTS

INTRODUCTION

A ship in the harbor is safe,
but that is not what the ships are built for.
John A. Shedd

You may not realize it, but you have unbelievable potential! The problem is, I can think of two places that are full of individuals with unbelievable, yet unrealized potential; prison yards and grave-yards... which leads me to ask a couple of questions: 1- Are you currently living up to your God-given potential? 2- Have you been accomplishing everything that God uniquely gifted and created you for? If the answer to either or even both of those questions is no, don't worry, you're not alone!

I am sure at one time or another, all of us have thought, felt, or even wondered aloud if there wasn't more to our lives than what we are experiencing. More to: your relationships, your reality, your faith, your fitness, your career, your Christianity, your dreams, your goals, your daily grind, your parenting, your prayers, and definitely more to your paycheck. And if you're honest more to the life you've been given and the life you are living, right?

That is because whether you realize it or not, you were made and meant for more! But do not take my word for it, God's Word declares it. He says you are an overcomer,[1] more than a conqueror,[2] you're created in God's image,[3] you're the head not the tail, above only and not beneath, you shall lend to many and not borrow,[4] and that you are God's workmanship.[5] I want to bring something to your attention, the Greek word for workmanship is *poiema*,[6] where we get the English word poem. Think about that for a moment. **That means you are an incredible, one-of-a-kind poem from Almighty God!**

This book is geared at helping you unlock and achieve your full God-given potential. It is going to confront childish mindsets, as well as challenge all excuses, procrastinations, and going through the motions faiths or lifestyles that are holding you back from the abundant life that God has promised you. There will be lots of personal and powerful stories that are geared at illustrating a specific spiritual truth or principle. At the end of each chapter there will be challenges: *Pause And Consider This* <u>points to ponder</u> and *Personally Apply Central Truth* <u>points to apply</u>. These are meant to push, prod, and propel you towards the blessed, fruitful, joy-filled life that God has called and created you to live! Work through them carefully and consider them like a **PACT** you are making with yourself and with God to challenge yourself and start *Putting Away Childish Things*!

Here's the thing, if you don't strive for more, then you will end up settling for less! In fact, in the Bible Jesus says to, "Strive to enter through the narrow door."[7] The Greek word for strive is *agonizomai* which literally means to agonize over; to exert oneself earnestly; or to fight or contend with an adversary.[8] This paints a powerfully accurate visual of the very real opposition you are going to face in this fight to reach your full potential. Especially in light of the Scripture that describes our "adversary the devil, as a roaring lion, walketh about, seeking whom he may devour."[9] Take heart though, despite his lies to the contrary, our adversary is not God's equal. He is a fallen angel,[10] not a fallen God, and truth be told, he is an already defeated foe.[11]

With that being said, I invite you to embark with me on an incredible journey. With any journey, the first step is always the hardest. You also need to know that there will be some obstacles, distractions, and unforeseen problems that are going to arise that will challenge your resolve along the way. So, buckle up, it is going to be a bumpy ride! But you will never discover new oceans (or your true God-given potential) until you have the courage to launch out and lose sight of the familiar shoreline.[12]

The fact that you picked up this book tells me that you are seriously ready for a change! But change, like success, doesn't come accidentally or automatically. I don't know about you, but I'd hate to stand before God only to have Him show me the life I could have lived, the difference I could have made, and the impact I could have had on my children, co-workers, church, and community if I had only believed God and lived up to my full potential.

The good news is that it is not too late! You can still become who you were made and meant to be, but time is ticking, and tomorrow is not promised to anyone. You have already taken a bold step of faith. Will you take another? If so, we have got some work to do, so let's get started!

CHAPTER 1

WHERE ARE YOU?

Then the Lord God called to the man,
and said to him, "Where are you?"
Genesis 3:9 NASB

I was blessed to have been adopted as a baby by two amazing parents. My dad was born in Pennsylvania and my mom was born in Wisconsin, both during the Great Depression (some of you reading this may have to google "Great Depression" so you will know what I am talking about). My dad was quite an imposing figure. He was 6'5", 240lbs, and by all accounts an old school "man's man", meaning he was a hardworking, no nonsense, didn't whine, cry, or show a lot of emotions kind of guy who wasn't big on saying, "I love you." My mom was an incredibly selfless woman who always put the needs of me and my sister above her own. She had the most important job in the world. She was a stay-at-home wife and mother (with the way things are today, some of you may have to google that as well).

My dad served for over 20 years in the military. Later, he worked 12-16 hours a day at a construction company that he started, to make sure that we never went without like he had as a child. Needless to say, I spent a lot of time with my mother. When mom wasn't dragging me to church, making the most incredible meals from scratch, or taking me to my ball games (and being my #1 fan), she loved to do work in her garden. Little did I know it would be in that garden with my mom that I would learn a life lesson and spiritual truth that would stay with me to this day.

I must admit that despite loving my mom dearly, I would often cut corners on the yard work she would ask me to do; especially, when it came to doing the weeding. In my defense, the other kids in my neighborhood would seemingly always have a kickball game they needed me to play, a go-kart they needed me to help build, or an adventure they needed me to go on. So, in my haste, instead of digging up the whole weed, I would often cheat and just quickly trim or pull off the top. Then I would try to hide the rest by throwing dirt on or covering them with a rock. But somehow, despite my best efforts to conceal my work (or lack thereof), mom would always know that I hadn't done what she had asked. After a while I started to think she had some kind of special X-Man X-ray vision or Supermom powers.

One day I finally got up the courage to ask mom how she always knew that I was cutting corners. She took me out to the garden and showed me that all the weeds I had supposedly pulled had popped back up. In that moment I finally got it. When you do not get to the root of the weeds, they always find their way back to the surface. The same is true with the issues in our lives.[1] So, what better place to start to get to the root of things that continue to pop back up in our lives and that are hindering us from reaching our God-given potential than the Garden of Eden.

You don't have to be a Bible scholar to know or at least have heard of what took place in that original garden, and how that drastically and dramatically altered the course of all mankind. We tend to focus a lot on the question that the serpent asked in the garden, "Has God really said"[2] and rightfully so. This subtle, seemingly insignificant question helped plant the seeds of doubt about the reliability of God's Word. Sadly, it has also led many into believing the lie that they can decide for themselves what God meant by what He said, and whether or not to take heed to His Word.

Amid all that was going on, it is easy to lose sight of the fact that God asked a question in the garden as well. I don't know about you, but I tend to sit up and take notice when an all-powerful, all-knowing, ever-present God asks a question. I think it is pretty safe to say that God didn't ask, "Where are you?" because He didn't know where His children were, but more likely to see if <u>they</u> knew where they were? Or more simply put, why weren't they where God expected them to be, and doing what God had created them to do? Could it be that God is asking some of you that very same question today?

You might be wondering how all this pertains to maximizing your God-given potential? Good question. First off, in order to achieve anything, or get anywhere in life, you will first need to know where you are starting. You would not load up the station wagon and take your family on a Chevy Chase style, cross-country vacation without first knowing where you were, secondly where you were going, and lastly without knowing how you were going to get to your desired destination, right? Unless of course you were my father, who would seemingly always get us lost in the middle of nowhere because he was too stubborn to ask for directions. I can picture a few of you nodding your heads because you know someone like this.

The reason why most shopping malls or large office buildings have a map with an "X" and the words "You Are Here" is because it makes it easier to find your way to your destination.

The other reason we are spending all this time discussing what took place in the Garden of Eden, is so we can get to the root of how we got to where we are in the first place. I am sure we have all heard it said that those that don't learn from history are destined to repeat it. The

Bible is way more than just a history book about mankind's sin. In fact, God proclaims it to be *HIS*-story to redeem, reconcile, and restore sinful mankind. Genesis, simply put, is the "book of beginnings" and gives us some serious insight into helping us identify the origins of the unhealthy and childish patterns of behavior that we can still fall back into when we are caught or confronted with our sin.

As any parent will tell you, the one thing they never had to teach their kids was how to disobey. I can hear parents everywhere saying, "Amen!" Especially ones with younger children. They know, as the Bible proclaims that even in the best of kids, "foolishness is bound in the heart of a child."[3] Sadly, through Adam's disobedience we were born into a sinful world and have a sin nature.[4] That is why we must learn to be obedient.[5] It is also why Jesus said we must be born again to enter or see the Kingdom of God,[6] but I'll talk about that in more detail later on. For now, let us go back to the garden and take a look at some of the ways we childishly avoid dealing with our sin and its consequences.

> *And the eyes of them both were opened, and they*
> *knew that they were naked; and they sewed fig leaves*
> *together, and made themselves aprons.*
> Genesis 3:7

1- THE COVER-UP

Should we be surprised that the first response of Adam and Eve was to try and cover what they did? Isn't that what we do also? There is a reason whenever we see a massive effort to avoid detection on the nightly news it is called a "cover-up". There is also a reason that most criminal activity and sinful behaviors take place at night, under the cover of darkness. The problem with that is that our sin will always come to light,[7] and Scripture says that whoever covers sin will not prosper.[8] It is also interesting that the couple tried to clothe themselves. Clothing in the Bible often represents righteousness[9] or right standing with God. You need to know though, that all our attempts of attaining righteousness or trying to clothe ourselves are nothing but filthy rags[10] in the eyes of a Holy God. That is why God had to intercede and clothe them in the blood of a freshly slain sacrifice because without the shedding of blood, there is no remission of sin.[11] This was a foreshadowing of what Christ would do for us later on the cross.

And they heard the voice of the Lord God
walking in the garden in the cool of the day:
And Adam and his wife hid themselves from
the presence of the Lord God amongst the
trees of the garden.
Genesis 3:8

2- HIDE-N-GO-SEEK

Do you remember playing hide-n-go-seek as a kid? I used to play all the time with the kids from the neighborhood. As I recall we had some really creative hiders back in the day. Kids will be kids though, so occasionally we would have a few "cheaters" that would duck inside their parent's house to hide. My most vivid memory of those times however, was of little Timmy who lived across the street from me. Timmy was a super friendly kid, always smiling, basically the kind of kid you love to hang out with. What made him so memorable though was the fact that he was a terrible hider. I am talking about trying to hide behind a tiny bush or just laying down in the grass ten feet away from the person looking for him. Again, great kid, just a terrible hider. I only mention little Timmy because after reading the Scripture above, Timmy has been surpassed by Adam and Eve, as the worst hide-n-go-seek players of all time. How are you going to hide from Almighty God, and behind some trees no less? David laments to God in the Psalms, "Where can

I go from thy Spirit?" Or "Where can I flee from thy presence?" He further goes on to basically say that if he ascended to Heaven, or made his bed in hell, God was there.[12]

The garden is not the only place where we find people that are hiding in plain sight. There are plenty of mainstream positions, platforms, podiums, places, political parties, and yes even pews/pulpits that people are hiding behind. For example, there are doctors and other PHD's hiding drug and alcohol addictions behind their prestigious degrees; professional athletes and polished actors/actresses that are hiding deep seeded insecurities and scandalous activities behind their awards, achievements, and accolades; CFO's and CEOs who are hiding serious debts and financial struggles behind their company's corporate success; soccer moms hiding their depression and eating disorders; PTA dads hiding adultery, anger, and abuse behind their meticulously kept yards and white picket fences; church parishioners who are hiding worry and worldly living behind their faithful church attendance; and regrettably, there are even Pastors and Priests hiding their frequenting of prostitutes, pornography, pedophilia, or the perverting of God's Word behind their lofty pulpits and perches. Although, unlike Adam, Eve, and little Timmy they have all gotten exceptionally good at hiding.

And the man said, The woman whom thou gavest
to be with me, she gave me of the tree, and I
did eat. And the Lord God said unto the woman, What
is this that thou hast done? And the woman said, The
serpent beguiled me, and I did eat.
Genesis 3:12-13

3- THE BLAME GAME

I cannot help but notice a lot of people playing the "blame game" these days. It doesn't seem to matter what the issue is, someone or something is always to blame. See if any of the following list doesn't sound like the usual suspects people claim as everything that is wrong with the world these days: guns, gangs, video games, violence on TV, Russians, republicans, school shootings, social security, aliens, illegal aliens, democrats, drones, nukes, North Koreans, the internet, identity theft, hurricanes, health care, prescription opioid use, police brutality, taxes, terrorists, technology, government waste, global warming, fake news, and reality TV shows. I think you get the point.

After saying all that, does it really come as any surprise that the blame game was taking place in the garden? In fact, it started there. Adam blamed Eve (even God) and Eve blamed the serpent. Eve basically used the all too familiar "devil made me do it" defense. The problem with that is it was a lie back then, and it is still a lie today. The devil cannot make you do anything. He only has the power to influence our choices, not determine them. It is interesting that the Scriptures refer to the devil as a serpent in Genesis, but as a dragon in the book of Revelation.[13] What happened that caused him to be so much bigger? Simply put, we fed him. Take comfort in the fact that when the pro-verbial curtain is pulled back on him, similar to the Wizard of Oz, the devil will be fully exposed, mocked, and questioned as "is this the one that made the earth to tremble, and shook kingdoms?"[14]

Then we have Adam. He not only blames the woman, but if you read closely, he throws blame at God as well, with the whole "that woman you gave me" line. Today is no different. There are many that are quick to question, accuse, or shake their fist at God for every problem in their lives, even blame Him for all the evil and suffering in the world. Amazing isn't it, how quickly we lose sight not only of God's love and mercy, but His goodness and grace as well? How about the fact that He is the one that gave us life in the first place, and that He views everything from an eternal and heavenly perspective? A Heaven that He created by the way, where there is no sin, sickness, sadness, or suffering,[15] because He is coming back to do away with all that. How many of us have ever stopped to think, before blaming and judging God, that if He were to eradicate all evil from the world right now, how many of us would be left standing?

I say all this because we live in a world that in many ways has abandoned personal accountability. In fact, if we were to take a real, honest look at a lot of the bad things in our lives, I think we'd quickly discover that it wasn't God chastening or punishing us; and most times it wasn't even an attack of the devil (although he is out to steal, kill, and destroy us,[16] which I'll go into more detail about in Chapter 4, *Identifying Our Enemy*). But the sad truth is most of the bad stuff in the world, or in our lives is a direct result of our sinful, rebellious nature and we are really just illustrating the biblical principle of "reaping what we sow".

I know I have thrown a lot at you in this first chapter, but hang in there, we are going somewhere. Plus, it is only when we learn the lessons from Adam and Eve in the garden and we get to the root of our issues and quit covering, hiding, and blaming others (including God) for our sin and struggles, that we can truly begin to take that huge first step toward achieving and operating at our full God-given potential... **as you cannot conquer or even correct what you will not confess and confront.**

If God were to ask you today "Where are you" how would you answer?

Are you where God expects you to be, and doing what He called you to do?

If not, why not?

Wherever you are now doesn't dictate how far you can go, it only determines where you start from. So, with that said, I would like for you to prayerfully and honestly examine where you are in the following aspects of your life:

- Faith
- Finances
- Marriage/Relationships
- Work/Ministry
- Freedom from sin

The Bible says, "Write the vision and make it plain on tablets, that he may run who readeth it."[17] Please take a moment and write out a brief picture of what it would look like to be living up to your full God-given potential in each of the areas listed above. Once we get a clear picture of where we are and where we are trying to get to, then we can begin to take some steps towards reaching that destination.

CHAPTER 2

I'M NOT THAT BAD, AM I?

And Jesus said unto him,
Why callest thou me good?
there is none good but one, that is, God.
Mark 10:18

D o you consider yourself to be a good person? This is something I have asked countless individuals while sharing my faith and witnessing for Christ. I really like the question for a number of reasons. For one, it gets people to hit the pause button for a moment and look at the kind of person they are, as well as the kind of life they are living. But, I've also found that it gives people the opportunity to open up and talk about their favorite subject- themselves!

So, what is your answer? Is it yes or I think so? In my own unscientific research, I have found that 9 out of 10 people I asked that question answered, "Yes" that they would say that they are a good person. That pretty much confirms the Scripture that says most people will proclaim their own goodness.[1] How is it though, with so many "good people" running around, that every time I turn on the news or read the paper, all I see is evil in the world? Murder, robbery, kidnapping, assault, child abuse, domestic violence, lying, cheating, theft, drunk driving, cruelty, slander, starvation, oppression, persecution, neglect, and slavery. Something is not adding up here!

Which brings me to my first point, **good compared to what**? There is a story about a family driving through the beautiful state of Montana in the fall. As they drive by a ranch the little girl in the back seat says, "Mama, look how bright white the sheep are!" Months later, as winter has now set in and the family travels past the same ranch, the little girl exclaims, "Ooh mama, look how dirty the sheep are!" Here we have the same ranch, the same sheep, and the same little girl, only two completely different narratives about the sheep. What changed? Did the sheep take a mud bath or suddenly dye their wool? Nope. All that had changed was what the sheep were being compared to. In the fall the grass was green, and the leaves were turning, so naturally, compared to that backdrop the sheep looked really white and clean. Come winter though, the snow had fallen and covered everything, so now those very same sheep compared to the pure, white, pristine backdrop didn't look so white or clean. The same is true for us; in that what we compare ourselves to matters.

Let me demonstrate. Take a moment and rate yourself on a scale of 1-10 in the following areas of your life: (Change to: 1=Help, I've got a lot of work to do, and 10=I've got this, in fact my book will be out next week):

Loving 1, 2, 3, 4, 5, 6, 7, 8, 9, 10
Kind 1, 2, 3, 4, 5, 6, 7, 8, 9, 10
Forgiving 1, 2, 3, 4, 5, 6, 7, 8, 9, 10
Patient 1, 2, 3, 4, 5, 6, 7, 8, 9, 10

Got your numbers for each one? How did you do? Good in some areas, not so good in others? Or are you above average in all categories? OK, now I am going to ask you to rate yourself again, only this time I want you to rate how loving, kind, forgiving, and patient you are compared to Jesus? So, did your numbers go up or down? They went down, huh? That is probably because your first rating was based on how you felt you are compared to everyone else, or your own standard of love, kindness, forgiveness, and patience, right? Once we put Jesus in the mix, who by the way is the perfect example and standard for all those qualities, it changes your whole perspective.

See, when people would tell me they thought that they were a good person, what they really meant was, "*I am not that bad, am I? At least not as bad as most people.*" There is a reason the Bible tells us those that measure themselves or compare themselves by themselves are not wise.[2] This mentality is nothing new. Jesus gave a parable (which is basically just a simple story used to illustrate a moral or spiritual lesson) about a Pharisee that thanked God that he was not as bad as other men because he did some "churchy stuff" and they were "sinners". In that same parable, there was a tax collector that would not even lift his eyes toward Heaven, but humbled himself, acknowledged that he was a sinner, asked for God's mercy, and received it.[3] That is the problem with comparing our sin to others, we quickly lose sight of the fact that in the eyes of a Holy God, we have all sinned and fallen short of His glory.[4] And the wages of that sin is death.[5]

Which brings me to my second point, **what is good**? Funny isn't it, how words can lose their significance when misused or even overused. Good is one of those words. Stop and think for a moment about all the things that we call "good" these days? That was a good sandwich, we went to a good party, she looks really good, this is a very good book (sorry, had to throw that one in there), he made a good catch, that was some good weed, you're good to go, or my girlfriend and I had a good time last night. Then we turn around and say, "God is good." See what I mean? We definitely live in an age that calls "evil good and good evil."[6]

Case in point- movies. Have you ever told someone about a really good movie you just saw? Then as you reflect on it you begin to realize that the "good movie" you are talking about had a whole lot of graphic violence, cheating, lying, idol worship, glorifying of promiscuous sexual behavior, and oh yeah it used the name of God (who gave us life) in vain or as a curse word over 30 times. Haven't I pretty much just described most movies that *unholy*-wood pumps out every year? And we think life doesn't imitate art or movies? Just turn on the news or read a newspaper and you will quickly see what I mean.

Feeling some conviction? Me too. If not, then you are probably dismissing or downplaying the effect that kind of stuff can have on you, which is something that a lot of people do these days. I mean, if we really think we can just allow ourselves to be bombarded with countless images of sex, violence, and sin every day and not have it desensitize us to evil, or even just lower the bar on what we think of as socially acceptable, normal, or good; we are deceiving ourselves.

This brings me to my last point, **God's goodness test**. When we are not measuring how good we are compared to others, or lowering the bar on what is good so we can leap over it, most of us base our goodness on the misguided belief that we are good as long as we do more good than bad. Am I right? As if that in and of itself somehow balances out the universal scales of justice.

Let me point out the obvious flaw with that logic. Imagine a person that has been a pillar in the community his whole life; always helping, giving, and doing for others. Then one day this same person that has done so much good for so many others starts having money problems and decides to rob a bank. During the course of this robbery, the individual shoots and kills a young security guard, who is a husband and father of two little children. The person is quickly caught, convicted, and stands before the judge for sentencing. Do you think that the judge will just let the person go free because of his lifetime of good deeds, as if that somehow outweighs this one, terribly bad deed? Of course not. If this judge is a fair and just judge, then justice demands that he hands down a swift and severe punishment for this offense, right? Do you really think it will be any different with a just and Holy God?

This brings me to what God has set forth as His standard of goodness for us, the Ten Commandments. Before I proceed any further, I have to ask, can you name all Ten Commandments? Once again, you are not alone if you can't. Sadly, a lot of people can name more Kardashians, than Commandments. That is because they are more interested in "keeping up with the Kardashians" than keeping the Commandments.

Now don't get nervous, but for this next section I am going to give you a brief synopsis of the Ten Commandments, and then a short "goodness" test. Yeah, I know, no one told you that there would be tests. Sorry, but I promise it will be a short one, four to five questions max. I am sure your brain has already been running through the Sunday school classes or the old school *The Ten Commandments* movie they show every Easter weekend, hoping some of the Commandments stuck. You are probably also thinking that you haven't killed anyone or slept with someone that's married, you have been to church before, have a Bible (somewhere), and have done your best to honor your mother and father, so you are good. Oops, there is that "good" word again. Are you ready? Oh yeah, I almost forgot. As I give you a summary of the Commandments, I am also going to give you a short number association with each Commandment. It really helped me to remember the Commandments front to back, and back to front, so hope it helps you as well.

<u>TEN COMMANDMENTS- Exodus 20:3-17</u>

1– Have no other gods before God. (Make God #1)

2– Do not make any idols of anything, and don't bow down or worship them. (When you look at the number 2, it looks like someone bowing down to worship. #2 don't bow to idols.)

3– Do not take the Lord's name in vain. (Picture the back of the number 3 as lips. #3 reminds us not to use the Lord's name in vain.)

4– Remember the Sabbath day to keep it holy. (The number 4 looks like a cross. #4 remember the Sabbath).

5– Honor your father and mother. (A hand has 5 fingers, picture holding your mom/dad's hand. #5 honor your mother and father).

6– Do not kill. (The number 6 looks like a bomb with a fuse. #6 don't kill).

7– Do not commit adultery. (Picture a broken heart with a 7 in the middle. #7 don't commit adultery).

8– Do not steal. (If you turn the 8 sideways it looks a burglar's mask. #8 don't steal).

9– Do not bear false witness. (Picture a 9 lying on a bed. #9 don't lie/bear false witness).

10– Do not covet. (Picture 10 as a $10 bill. #10 don't covet other's stuff).

So hopefully next time you think of the Ten Commandments, you will picture #6 (a bomb with a fuse, don't kill), #8 (burglars mask, don't steal), or #1 (make God #1), etc. Alright, now that we have brushed up on the Commandments, let's get to the test.

GOD'S GOODNESS TEST:

1– Have you ever told a lie? (even a little one)

2– Have you ever stolen anything? (even something small)

3– Have you ever used God's name as a curse word? (This includes God, Jesus, even Holy as "Holy is His name."[7])

4– Have you ever looked at someone with lust? (Jesus says to do so is the same as committing adultery with them in your heart.[8])

5– Have you ever had hate for someone? (God equates hate for a person as murder.[9])

Yeah, I know, God's ways aren't our ways. So, how did you do? How many did you answer yes to? Two? Three? Four? All five? Hard to hear that we are all lying, thieving, blaspheming, adulterers, and murderers at heart, isn't it? And just think that was only five of the Commandments! But it is even harder to fathom that we are all going to stand before and be judged by a Holy God.[10] Will you be innocent or guilty on that day? Will it be Heaven or hell for all eternity? Even if you only broke one of the Commandments like lying, the Word of God declares that whoever breaks even one of the Commandments is guilty of breaking them all.[11]

This explains why the Psalms say that "God looked down from heaven upon the children of men, to see if there were any that did understand, that did seek God. Every one of them is gone back, they are altogether become filthy; there is none that doeth good, no, not one."[12]

O taste and see that the Lord is good.
Psalm 34:8

Do you have a favorite meal? If so, I am sure there is a certain spot or better yet a certain someone that makes that meal like no one else, am I right? For me it is my mom's chicken, cornbread, and cobbler, all made from scratch. Nothing else compares or even comes close. In fact, it is so amazing that it pretty much has ruined me from eating anyone else's, even KFC's or Popeye's. I only say that because the same is true of God. We have spent a fair amount of time looking at what we call and consider good. We even took a hard look at our own level of goodness. Despite what we may think is good, or how good we may think we are, one thing is certain, **God is Good**! You don't have to take my word for it, like with my mom's cobbler; you can taste and see for yourself.

If it is alright with you, I'm going to flip the script for a moment and give you some good news, amen? God is a Good Shepherd.[13] He withholds no good thing from those who walk uprightly.[14] He causes all things to work together for the good to those who love Him.[15] He wants you to eat the good of the land.[16] And truth be told, it is His goodness that leads you to repent, and change the way you think and live.[17] In fact, that is what the word *Gospel* means, *Good News*!

If you, despite being evil, know how to give
good gifts to your children, how much more
will your Father who is in heaven give good
things to those who ask Him!
Matthew 7:11 NKJV

YOU ARE GIFTED

While we are on the subject of good news, do you know that God has blessed you with some amazing gifts? Oh, they may not be the glamorous athletic or artistic abilities that so many idolize or long for, but you are gifted just the same. Perhaps you are a gifted salesperson (got the gift of gab), which often equates to being called to preach or evangelize, just saying. Perhaps your gift is being extremely patient or a good listener (oh those are gifts, as most people don't listen, they just wait to speak), this often coincides with being a teacher or counselor. Or just maybe you are the only person at work that can get that finicky copier or new computer program to work right. Whatever it is you can be sure of this, you have got unique gifts, and as the Scripture says, "Every good and perfect gift is from above."[18]

Have you ever received a gift card for your birthday or the holidays? I recently read that many of those gift cards go unused, resulting in billions of dollars of potential gifts and blessings just wasted. Why is this? Maybe over time the individuals that received the gift cards just forgot about the gift they had been given. Maybe they were just too busy (or lazy) to do what it took to get something out of the gift. Or maybe, they downplayed or didn't fully recognize the value of the gift they had been given. See the thing about a gift is it must not only be received but redeemed to realize its full potential. The way I look at it is simple; the unique talents, abilities, and potential each of us possesses are God's gifts to us. What we then do with those abilities is our gift back to God. Sadly, far too many people have not recognized or are not utilizing their gifts to their full potential. Even sadder is that some are misusing or even perverting their gifts for personal gain, glory, or often unwittingly for the god of this world, who has taken them captive to do his will.[19]

This is probably why the Word encourages us to stir up the gifts of God,[20] and warns us not to neglect them.[21] If all that wasn't amazing enough, there's more! If you are a born again, Spirit-filled, follower of Jesus, then you have also been blessed with the following: The gift of righteousness,[22] the gift of the Holy Spirit,[23] the gift of eternal life,[24] and a diversity of amazing spiritual gifts.[25]

Have you recognized and identified what your specific gifts are yet? If so, are you operating in them? The thing is you will never truly experience the abundant, joy-filled life that God has for you until you do!

After reading this, whose standard of "good" are you living by? Yours, the world's, or God's?

What have you been calling good that you now realize is not?

If you haven't identified the gifts that God has specifically blessed you with, prayerfully ask God to reveal them to you.

If you have identified them, what are some specific ways you can honor God with your gifts?

CHAPTER 3

CONSIDER YOUR WAYS

Now therefore thus saith the
Lord of Hosts; Consider your ways.
Haggai 1:5

There is an old story about a ship's Captain, who on a foggy night saw what appeared to be the light of another ship heading straight towards him. He quickly had the communications officer signal to the other ship to, "Alter your course ten degrees south." A little while later a reply came back, "Alter your course ten degrees north." Furious, the Captain then had his communications officer send a second message, "I am a Captain in the United States Navy, alter your course ten degrees south right now." Again a few minutes passed, the response came, "I am a volunteer in the Merchant Marines; alter your course ten degrees north right now." The Captain, now totally enraged had this final message sent, "I command you to alter your course ten degrees south immediately, as I am on a battleship!" Shortly after the Captain of the U.S. battleship Arizona received the following reply, "Sir I strongly recommend that you change course ten degrees north immediately, as I am in a lighthouse!" The moral of this story; failure to not only consider, but change your ways can have devastating consequences.

So, let me ask you something. When is the last time you really took a moment to consider the way you are living? For this next chapter we are going to pause and shine some light on the way we do things, as well as to compare and contrast our ways versus God's ways. Sounds a little intimidating, I know but trust me it is one of those necessary stops we need to make if we are going to get to where we want to be.

In today's society it seems like a lot of what we do on a daily basis is largely influenced by or based off of three main factors:

- Culture –Everyone is doing it.
- Emotion –I felt like doing it.
- Tradition- I have always done it.

But the question is, are those really reliable guides to follow? Let's stop and take a closer look.

CULTURE- Everyone is doing it!

For starters the word culture has the word "cult" in it, which to me immediately brings to mind images of some really misled, outraged groups of people that I wouldn't ever want to follow. Plus, I have always been a big believer that those who follow the crowd tend to get lost in it. On a more serious note, the main problem with doing things based on what everyone else is doing is that their standard is always changing. Case in point, think back on some of the crazy things that have generally been "culturally" accepted at different times: gunfights to settle disputes, slavery, the world is flat (sorry to offend any that still hold fast to that opinion), cannibalism, feeding Christians to lions, and using leaches as a medical treatment; just to name a few.

We look back on all that and say that was crazy or what were people thinking, but at the time, all of that was widely accepted as the cultural norm. The thing is, I don't even need to look back 100+ years or at remote cultures around the globe to see crazy stuff going on. I look around at some of the things that have been or are currently considered culturally acceptable right here, right now, in the good old US of A and I have to shake my head. They don't call it "culture shock" for nothing. If all that still doesn't convince you that culture is not a reliable role model let me echo the timeless wisdom of mothers throughout history: "If everyone jumped off a bridge, would you?" Sadly, the answer for many today would be "yes".

EMOTION- I felt like doing it!

I must confess there have been days that I did not feel like going to work or even getting out of bed (you too, huh?). I am also not proud to admit that there have even been times as a Christian that I did not feel like forgiving or praying for someone that had wronged me (hey, put those stones down, just being honest). But you know what, I went to work, forgave, and prayed anyways. Does that make me a hypocrite? Absolutely not! Like countless others around the world, and even some that are reading this book, I did what I was supposed to do and what God expected me to do. Why, because I live by faith, not by feelings.

I hate to break this to you, but doing stuff based solely off how you feel is a sure-fire way to end up someplace you don't want to be. Just think back for a moment on all the wrong words you've spoken, wrong roads you've taken, and wrong decisions you've made. I will bet that there were some strong emotions attached to each of those decisions, correct?

Have you ever said, "I love you" to someone and then six months later you cannot stand the person? This is a perfect example of how flawed, faulty, and even fickle feelings can be at times. In a world that is so wrapped up in self-awareness, self-help, self-gratification, and yes... even selfies, can you imagine how bad things would be if everyone only did what they felt like doing? Plus, just think about all the things that can impact and affect our feelings and emotions; illness, hunger, bad news, bills, rush hour traffic, lack of sleep, etc. Isn't it time to quit doing things off how we feel and start doing them based on God's truth revealed in His Word?

TRADITION- I have always done it!

Did you have any family traditions growing up? I am sure many of us have heard the story of the husband that brings his wife a large ham for the holidays. She cuts the ends off and preps it to cook for dinner. The husband after seeing his wife do this asks her why she cut off the best part of the ham. The wife replies, "I don't know, that's how my mom always did it." Perplexed the husband has his wife call her mom and ask her why she cut the ends off the ham off before cooking it. The mom says, "I don't know, that's how my mom always did it." Now curious the wife calls her grandmother and asks her why she cut off the ends of the ham before cooking it. Grandma laughs and simply says, "I don't know why you guys are cutting off the ends of the ham, but I did it so it would fit in the pan."

This is not to say all traditions are bad or wrong, but the story really does illustrate the point about how many things we do a certain way, basically out of tradition, and don't even know why we are doing them. As funny as that sounds, it can also be extremely dangerous. That is why the Apostle Paul warned the church at Colossae not to be taken captive through philosophy and vain deceit, according to the "tradition of men."[1] Even Jesus rebuked the religious leaders about making the "commandment of God of none effect by their tradition."[2]

Let's face it; we are all definitely creatures of habit. From the time we wake up, until we lay our head on the pillow again, many of the routines we have developed over time are just repeated over and over again. It is almost as if we lived our lives on a loop, like in the Bill Murray movie *Groundhog Day*. Think about the autopilot way we go through each day. You wake up, shave, shower (or wash your face), brush your teeth, comb your hair, if you are my wife you spend an hour on your make-up, and then get dressed (I don't know about you, but for me it's always left sock first, then right, left pant leg, then right pant leg). Then it's a quick breakfast and probably for a lot of you reading this it is also the daily battle of getting the kids fed, dressed, and off to school. Then there is probably some kind of commute, right? After that I would imagine that most of you work somewhere between 6–16 hours a day, depending on the type of job you have. A lot of days probably include the usual workplace griping, gossiping, and personal drama, right? Then another commute back home (hopefully without any horn honking or inappropriate hand gestures), another shower, dinner, and then get caught up on how your significant other and kids' day went. Then maybe catch a little of the news, probably something technology related, a favorite TV show you watch each week, then whatever bedtime routine you have. Hopefully, during all that you are taking time out each day for some prayer, Bible reading, giving of thanks, and helping others. Although, if you are not careful, even that can become just another "going through the motions" routine.

> *For my thoughts are not your thoughts,*
> *neither are your ways my ways, saith the Lord.*
> *For as the heavens are higher than the earth, so*
> *are my ways higher than your ways, and my*
> *thoughts than your thoughts.*
> Isaiah 55:8-9

GOD'S WAYS vs. OUR WAYS

Let's be honest. Most of us think that the way we do things (live, love, treat others, raise our kids, serve God, etc.) is just fine. But is it the best way, or more importantly the way that God wants us to do things? Probably not. "Every way of man is right in his own eyes."[3] We just spent some time looking at the stuff that influences the way that we do things. Now we are going to compare and contrast God's ways and our ways, so we can see where we are at versus where God wants us to be.

For the most part, the majority of us love those that love us. If we are honest, even that can be challenging at times, correct? But God, who is love,[4] not only loves those who love Him, but also loves those who curse, question, rebel against, and reject Him. Ponder that for a moment. I can hear some of you already saying, "Yeah, but He's God." Amazing how quickly we forget that God made us in His image and likeness,[5] as well as breathed His Spirit into us.[6] As incredible as that is, I don't think there is anything that more clearly illustrates just how different God's ways are from our ways than forgiveness.

Let's start with how we forgive. Let me ask you something. What is the worst thing that someone could do to you that you would forgive? Lie to you? Steal from you? Cheat on you? More? Less? How about beat you, spit on you, and nail you to a cross? Probably not, huh? Now, I want you to think about how many times could this individual or these individuals do that worst thing to you, and you would still forgive them? Once, twice, seven times? How about 70 x 7 times?[7] Is your standard for forgiveness different if the person who wronged you is a friend, family member, enemy, stranger, or brother/sister in Christ? Alright, last question and this is a big one, what would the person that wronged you have to do in order to earn or receive your forgiveness?

Now that I have given you a little something to chew on, let us take a couple minutes to look at how God forgives us for all the sins and offenses that we have committed in our lifetime. Consider the following:

If we confess our sins, He is faithful
and just to forgive us our sins, and to cleanse us
from all unrighteousness.
1 John 1:9

As far as the east is from the west, so far
hath He removed our transgressions from us.
Psalm 103:12

And their sins and iniquities
will I remember no more.
Hebrews 10:17

Who is a God like you, that pardons iniquity
and passes over the rebellious act of the remnant
of His possession? He does not retain His anger
forever, because He delights in unchanging love.
He will again have compassion on us; He will
tread our iniquities under foot. Yes, You will
cast all their sins into the depths of the sea.
Micah 7:18-19 NASB1995

SIN = To miss the mark, an offense.[8]
TRESPASS = Unintentional error or willful transgression.[9]
INIQUITY = Twisting or deliberately perverting.[10]

If you ever had any doubt about just how good and merciful God is, take a moment to reflect on the Scriptures we just read. Our sins forgiven and remembered no more. Our transgressions removed, and ALL our iniquities pardoned and cast into the depths of the sea! Unbelievable!

As this is such an important subject, I want to go even deeper to make sure you are really getting this. For starters just what is forgiveness anyway?

Forgiveness is not:
- reciting some half-hearted prayer or saying "I forgive you".
- pretending an offense didn't happen.
- condoning or turning a blind eye to a sin, hurt, or offense.
- forgetting what someone did.

Forgiveness is:
- agreeing with God that you need to forgive.
- surrendering the right to get even with someone.
- my letting go of the belief that the past will ever turn out differently and letting the prisoner go (only to find out that the prisoner was me).

I am sure I am not the only one who has ever struggled with forgiving. Usually, I would justify my not forgiving by telling myself that the person who wronged me was not really sorry and therefore didn't deserve to be forgiven. Sound familiar? I thought it would. But then I had to ask myself some tough questions. First, if God forgave like I did would I be forgiven? And second, did I deserve God's forgiveness?

I have heard it said that not forgiving is like drinking poison and hoping it would hurt someone else, or that not forgiving is like burning a bridge I must travel across one day. While I don't know about that, I do know what God says about not forgiving:

1– **Not forgiving is a sin.** The Scripture says that to know the good you are supposed to do, and then to not do it, is sin.[11] It also commands us that as Christ forgave us, we are to do also.[12] And as we all know, disobeying God is always a sin.

2– **Not forgiving keeps us from walking in the complete forgiveness of God.** This is a little more complex issue, so let me try and simplify it. I am assuming most of us know or have at least heard the *Lord's Prayer* before. But do you realize that right after that passage the Scripture says that "if we forgive not men their trespasses, neither will your Heavenly Father forgive your trespasses."[13] There are two aspects to forgiveness. The first is *positional forgiveness*. This is bestowed upon a sinner once and for all upon receiving Christ as their Savior and being born again. But there is also *relational forgiveness*." This, as a believer and a follower of Christ, would seem to indicate that not forgiving hinders a believer's fellowship/relationship with their Heavenly Father. Sadly, I know this all too well firsthand as there have been times that even after ALL God forgave me for, I still have struggled to forgive others, and in those times my intimacy with God has suffered.

3– **Not forgiving hinders your prayers from being answered.** Ever felt like your prayers were just bouncing off the ceiling? Me too. The Scriptures make a clear connection to the importance of forgiving or even reconciling with others, before coming to God.[14] So, if your prayers seem to not be getting heard, you might want to ask God to show if you are holding on to any ought, offense, or unforgiveness against another? A word of caution though, once God shows you something, He expects you to deal with it, even if it's uncomfortable.

4– **Not forgiving keeps you in torment.** Jesus tells a powerful story of a man who owed what today would amount to 60 million days wages. Basically, an insurmountable debt by any standard. The man and his family were about to be sold into slavery as a result of his debt (a powerful reminder of how our sin can negatively impact those we love). Desperate, the man pleaded with the King for mercy. Surprisingly, the King had compassion on him, released him, and forgave the debt! Pretty amazing, huh?

The thing is the man, rather than being grateful, went and sought out a fellow servant who owed him the equivalent of three months wages (a decent amount, but nothing in comparison to what he had owed). And despite all that he had been forgiven, he showed no mercy to the man that owed him. In fact, he choked him out and had him thrown in prison. When the King heard about how the man whose debt he had forgiven treated someone else in a similar situation, he was outraged and ordered the man to be turned over to the "tormentors" until he had paid all he owed. This passage then gives a sobering warning that likewise will our Heavenly Father do unto any of us if we do not forgive from our heart "everyone his brother their trespasses."[15]

5– **Not forgiving will turn on you.** There is also a powerful account in the book of Esther, in which a man named Haman gets offended by a man named Mordecai and plots to kill him. His bitterness runs so deep, that he devices a conspiracy to take out all the Jewish people, just because Mordecai, a Jew, would not bow or pay homage to him. Haman's bitterness leads him to build a gallows, 75 feet high to hang Mordecai from, but his lack of forgiveness ends up turning on him and he gets hung from his own gallows.

I think it is safe to say God takes not forgiving very serious, wouldn't you agree? But if all that still has not got you considering your ways, let me remind you of one more important piece of information; according to God's Word every way we do things is right in our own eyes.[16] It also goes on to say that there is a way that seems right to each of us, but its end is the way of death.[17] The undeniable truth is that at the end of the day everyone is going one of two ways, the right way or the wrong way. Our way or God's way. His Word says many find the broad way that leads to destruction,[18] and few find the straight and narrow way, that leads to life.[19] All that is a good reason to stop, take a moment, and seriously **CONSIDER YOUR WAYS**!

How has culture, emotion, or tradition affected the way that you do things?

Is the way you are currently living, loving, and forgiving God's way or your way?

After reading this chapter is there anyone that you are struggling to forgive? Maybe even yourself?

If so, will you be like the man that had been forgiven much, but refused to forgive? Or will you realize your need to forgive, confess your lack of forgiveness and before moving on to the next chapter, forgive as Christ forgave you?

CHAPTER 4

GROW UP ALREADY, WOULD YOU?
(I'LL NEVER BE LIKE MY PARENTS)

Growing old is inevitable, growing up is optional.
Edwin Cole

L et me ask you something, have you ever seen a grown man or woman acting, talking, or behaving like a child? Not a good look, is it? Perhaps you still have some childish behaviors, tendencies, or activities of your own that you need to work on? Hard to admit, I know, but if I am talking to you just look straight ahead and keep reading, no one will know.

Now, when I say childish behavior, I'm not talking about eating Gerber's in a highchair, playing in a sandbox, or walking around with a binky, blankie, or a sippy cup (by the way if you *are* doing any of those things, come on grow up already, would you?!) But if we can be honest with ourselves for a moment, many of us are still carrying around some childish mindsets and mannerisms. While these may seem harmless, if we dig a little deeper, I think we'll find that these childish behaviors are at the root of everything that we struggle with as a church, community, and country. Everything from growing divorce rates, generational rising debt, dangerous overeating and obesity, deadly opioid overdoses, out of control children, to overcrowded correctional complexes, (just to name a few). It is these juvenile, immature activities and attitudes that are not only hurting us spiritually and physically but are keeping us from living our best and blessed lives. So, let's stop and take a look at two aspects of our lives that are most impacted by childish actions and attitudes: our relationships and finances.

RELATIONSHIPS:

When is the last time you told someone to grow up, act your age, or quit being a baby? And you know I have to ask, when is the last time someone said that to you? Last year, last month, last night? By the way, if you are hearing any of those things on a regular basis you already know what I am going to say. Come on grow up already, would you?! Even if you haven't said it directly to someone, you've probably thought it about someone that was acting childish or throwing a temper tantrum. Funny thing is, someone has probably thought the same thing about each one of us at one time or another.

So, you may be asking how any of this negatively affects relationships. Let me explain. When I act childishly around my wife it causes her to instinctively respond by mothering me, and I don't know any woman that marries a man so she can mother him, or vice-a-versa. Then when I act childishly around my children, they begin to look at me as a peer or a partner, instead of as their parent. This can cause not only confusion, but a lack of confidence in my leadership, as well as undermine my parental authority and ability to speak into their lives. That whole "Do as I say, not as I do" mantra parents have been known to preach doesn't work. If they see you doing it and you are who they look up to, can you really be surprised if they follow in your footsteps? (The Little Man poem at the end of this chapter really highlights this point.)

Lastly, when I act childishly around my friends, they are often forced to try and scold or discipline me (aka parent me). Now, there are naturally going to be times in any friendship when my friend is going to have to tell me something I probably don't want to hear.[1] That is of course if they are a true friend. But my peers or my partners shouldn't have to babysit or parent me when I act like a child. Plus, it makes it harder for them to ever take me seriously when I am trying to give them wise counsel or a warning[2] about a mistake they are about to make. Yet we wonder why so many of our relationships are dysfunctional or in disarray.

FINANCES:

I am sure we can all remember as a child a certain gift, toy, or something that we just had to have, right? We hinted, begged, pleaded, pouted, probably even threw a tantrum or two until we finally got what we wanted. As a child the "got to have" items for me were a Slinky, an Etch A Sketch, Hot Wheels with a track, an Atari Pong game system (yes, I'm that old!), a GI Joe action figure with the Kung-Fu grip, and a BB gun (I know the whole "you'll shoot your eye out kid" line). The funny thing is that after a couple of weeks, most of those prized possessions were either beaten-up, blown-up, broken, or I had just gotten bored with them. Looking back, I would have been wise to have just left all those "got to have" things in their original packaging and never touched them. I could have retired by now, as I recently saw some of the Star Wars stuff I had back in the day going for thousands of dollars. In fact, even the $5 Scooby Doo lunch pail I used to lug to school every day was selling for $600 in mint condition, $1,000 if you had the thermos that went with it. Unbelievable!

I say all that because even though we are all grown-up now, many of us still carry around that same childish, "I've got to have it, can't live without it" mindset. This causes us to make immature, emotionally driven purchases, or basically buy things we don't need, with money we don't have, to impress people we don't know or really even like. All this to try and fill a void in our lives that only God can fill. Think I am wrong? Just take a look in your attic, shed, or closet and see how many things are in there, like that ab blaster, stair stepper, that 40th pair of shoes, or pretty much anything else you purchased from an infomercial or the home shopping network that is sitting around collecting dust.

If that is not proof enough that we still have some childish, impulsive mindsets that we need to address, let me ask you this: how much credit card debt do you have? For the record, the average American has approximately $6,270, but I am sure all of yours was for rent, groceries, and emergency purchases. Not so much, huh? Funny how quickly we will justify going $6,270 or so in debt, which with credit card interest rates the way they are, means by the time most people pay it off will probably cost them $11,000+. And for what, a bunch of stuff you just had to have now? Sounds like the kind of deal a desperate gambler would make with a loan shark, doesn't it? But hey, the credit card company is your friend, right? And they do give you a couple dollars back, plus a "free hat" or something, so you are getting over on them, right? Sorry for the sarcasm, but just trying to open some blind eyes to just how immature and irrational some of our money management skills are. We don't even want to take a look at where some of our worst financial decisions take place, on the showroom floor of a car dealership. Have to have that new car smell though, right? Who cares how much the car depreciates the moment that you drive it off the lot. But with our national debt over 28 trillion and counting, it is not hard to see where we learned it from. Sad how quickly we have lost sight of the biblical warning that the borrower is slave to the lender.[3]

I'LL NEVER BE LIKE MY PARENTS

How many kids have uttered these very same words at some time or another? This is no knock on parents; a lot of this is probably said out of temporary anger or frustration over our parent's rules or method of discipline. But then, as those of you with kids of your own know, we often find ourselves turning into our mothers and fathers later in life. There are even some hilarious commercials that make fun of this very point. If that wasn't proof enough, the Scriptures are full of examples of children following in their parent's footsteps, both good and bad. So why is this?

I can remember some hot summer days growing up and playing kickball with kids from the neighborhood. We usually didn't have any money for sodas or Slurpees, so one day I decided to make us all some Kool-Aid. Problem was my mom wouldn't let me bring any of her glassware or pitchers outside, so I had to improvise. All that I could find to mix the Kool-Aid in was an empty bleach jug.

I must have rinsed that thing out a hundred times with the hose and some dish soap that I had smuggled outside, until I could no longer smell even a hint of the bleach. I put a whole pack of strawberry Kool-Aid in the jug, along with a healthy amount of sugar and ice cubes, which I also had snuck out of the house. Then I shook it up really good. It didn't take long for us to realize that the refreshing strawberry drink that we had all been waiting for still had a funny taste to it. The reason being is that containers will often retain the taste of what has first been poured into them. Same principle is true of us as children.

That is why God designated and designed parents to be the first ones to pour into their children. Or as the Scripture says, to train them up in the way they should go, so when they are old, they won't depart from it.[4] Problem is that too many parents these days have abandoned, abused, or delegated this very solemn responsibility, and just as bad are all the parents out there that are still carrying around hurts, regrets, and disappointments from their own childhoods and are now trying to live vicariously through their kids. Not sure what I am talking about? Obviously, you haven't been to a peewee football game, little league baseball game, or even a children's beauty pageant lately. Believe me nothing is uglier than watching a bunch of adults screaming, squabbling, or even scrapping with the refs, umpires, judges, and other parents, while the kids look on. So, for you parents out there, what are you teaching your kids?[5] Are you practicing what you preach? Even more importantly, practicing what Jesus preached?[6] I wrote a short poem to my sons to remind myself that more than the words that I say, the number one way I will ever lead, guide, or teach my kids anything is by example:

Little Man

A careful man I must always be,
a little child follows me.
I know I dare not go astray,
for fear he'll go the selfsame way.

I cannot once escape his eyes,
whatever he sees me do he tries.
Like me he says he's going to be,
this little boy who looks up to me.

He listens when I talk or pray,
and believes in every word I say.
The worst in me he must not see,
this little fellow who is watching me.

I must be careful as I go,
that Christ in me to him I show.
For who I am shapes who he'll be,
this little man who looks just like me.

And I sought for a man among them, that
should make up the hedge, and stand in
the gap before me for the land, that I should
not destroy it: but I found none.
Ezekiel 22:30

GOD IS LOOKING FOR A MAN

For all the women out there reading this, by all means keep reading. But if you don't mind, I am going to spend a little time at the end of this chapter addressing the men out there. Believe me you will thank me later.

- How many of you are sons?
- How many of you are husbands?
- How many of you are fathers?
- Any grandfathers?
- How many of you are hoping to be husbands, fathers, and even grandfathers some day?
- OK, now for the real question, if you answered yes to any of those, how many of you are MEN??

I am sure that may seem like a silly question, in light of the questions I just asked, but we just read the Scripture above that God was looking for a man and found NONE!! That is because we have a lot of boys running around posing as men, as well as many that are trying to "be the man", without really knowing how to be a man. I can hear a lot of the women out there saying, "Amen!"

See when you came into the world, I highly doubt that the doctor or nurse that helped deliver you went and told your parents when you were born, "it's a man!" That is because men aren't born, they become. Probably why when King David was about to die, he charged his son

Solomon to be strong and shew himself a man.[7] Basically, telling him to "man up!" Solomon would later go on to write that the whole duty of a man is to fear God and keep His Commandments.[8] Later in the Scriptures the prophet Micah tells us exactly what God requires of men. It is simple, "to do justly, and to love mercy, and to walk humbly with thy God."[9] Is that you? Before you answer, we first need to get a better understanding of manhood. What does it mean to be a man? When and how do you become a man? And where do we get our views of manhood to begin with? So, if you are ready, let's get this party started.

WHEN DOES A BOY BECOME A MAN?

How would you answer that question? Is it a certain age, like 13, 16, 18, or 21? I think we all know that those are just numbers, as some individuals can be a man at 18, while others are regrettably still boys at 50. That is because while you are only young once, you can be immature a lifetime. Maybe you believe that boys become men after some specific event or rite of passage? So, does that mean you become a man when you learn how to drive a car, move out of your parent's house, get married, have sex for the first time, or when you become a father? Maybe it is when you get a job, start paying your own bills, go to prison, or grow a beard? (By the way, if that is what it takes, the beard part anyways, then I'm in trouble at 58 years old!) Or do you have to save a life, enlist in the military, or grab a lion by its tail for you to officially be "declared" a man? Still not sure, let me help you out. Scripture says, "When I was a child I spake as a child, I understood as a child, I thought as a child: but when I became a man, I put away childish things."[10] That equates biblical manhood with the *Putting Away of Childish Things*. Sound familiar?

The next logical question then has to be:

WHAT MAKES A MAN A MAN?

If you are old school like my father was, you would probably say the things that make a man are strength, toughness, a good work ethic, being a protector and provider, someone that's in charge, and always right. Sadly, most people's measuring stick of being a man these days is performance based. How much money he has, how many women he has slept with, how athletic he is, and how successful he is. Basically, the Four *B's*: Billfold, Bedroom, Ball Field, and Boardroom. Fortunately, God doesn't measure you by those things and is not moved or impressed by how hard you can hit, how far you can spit, or how many women or possessions you can get. Instead, He looks at your heart, humility, and honesty; your worship and witness; your service and surrender,; and above all your commitment, courage, and Christlikeness. So, if you are still unsure as to whether you are a boy or a man let me make the vision plain:

BOYS	MEN
Try and get their way	Trust in God's way
Blame others	Take responsibility
Do what feels right	Do what is right
Play a lot	Pray a lot
Live for today	Have a vision for the future

All of which leads me to ask the following:

- How many of you never knew your father?
- How many didn't grow up with a father in the home?
- How many did have a father in the home, but he wasn't a good role model?
- How many had a father that was incarcerated?

- How many have lost their father? (Me too, and my heart goes out to you for your loss)

If you answered yes to any of those questions above than I have to ask:

WHERE DID YOU LEARN HOW TO BE A MAN?

School or the streets? Partners, prison, or the Playboy channel? Maybe you learned how to be a man from the movies, magazines, or your mom? Believe me when I say that I mean no disrespect by that to all the amazing moms, aunties, grandmas, sisters, and women out there that have had to step up and fill the gap for the multitude of men that have either abused or just abandoned their fatherly duties and responsibilities. The truth is men need men to model real manhood. And, the real tragedy is, it wasn't that long ago that when a father passed away the whole community would mourn and come together to help raise the children. Nowadays, fathers just up and leave and no one even blinks an eye or sheds a tear. What has happened?

Do you know that 90% of major crimes are committed by men? And 85% of those men (or boys) didn't know their fathers, lost their fathers, or didn't have a father or a positive father figure in the home. Coincidence? I don't think so. In addition, when those same conditions exist, the chances a child will get killed, locked-up, be addicted to drugs, have a child as a teenager, or even commit suicide go up exponentially.

So, we started this section with God looking for a man and finding none. I can't help but wonder if God would find any men today? Not a boy, but a man. Not just any man, but a faithful man. A man with character and integrity. A man that will stand in the gap and build up a wall for his family, friends, children, and community, no matter what the cost. A man that will stay when others run, stand when others fall, shine when others cover and not compromise. A man that will not only love his family but lead them; not only pray for his family but pray with them; not only minister Christ but model His character. A man that will step up, stand up, speak up, wake up (if you are sitting down and this is speaking to you then you should probably be rising to your feet about now). Become a man that will own up, grow up, man up, and show up for his faith and his family! Is that you today? If so, would you make a bold new commitment and pray the following prayer:

Heavenly Father,

I have heard Your call to courageous manhood, and I'm responding to it. I commit to putting away ALL childish ways of thinking, talking, and living. Help me Lord to be the man that you called and created me to be. A man that stands up and speaks up for his faith and his family. From this day forward I will not look back, hold back, turn back, or stay silent any longer. I make this vow to you Lord, and to my wife, kids, family, church, and community. Please give me the strength to keep it and honor You.

In Jesus name, Amen!

> *Without Goals and a plan to reach them, you are*
> *like a ship that has set sail with no destination.*
> Fitzhugh Dodson

NEXT LEVEL/SMART PLAN

So far we have taken a look at some of the things that are hindering us from reaching our God-given potential. Now I would like to help give you a blueprint to start making those goals a reality. It is a straightforward, easy to put into practice method that you can apply to any goals that you are struggling to realize. I call it the **SMART Plan**.

S *pecific-* Exactly what are you trying to accomplish?

M *easurable-* What are some mile markers to track your progress along the way?

A *ccountable-* Share your goals/plan with someone that will hold you accountable.

R *ealistic-* Something God has shown you in His Word that can be achieved.

T *imely-* When do you expect it to be accomplished?

How has childish behavior impacted your life, finances, and relationships?

In what ways are you like your parents (good or bad)?

How is your definition of a man compared to God's?

Using the **SMART Plan**, what is a physical, spiritual, financial, or relationship goal that you want to accomplish so that you can be a blessing to others? (Possible examples are: being able to run five miles, getting out of debt, read and remember more Scripture, being more bold in sharing your faith, spending more quality time with your wife and children, etc.)

LOOKING BACK

And Jesus said unto him, No man,
having put his hand to the plough, and
looking back, is fit for the kingdom of God.
Luke 9:62

E ver ask yourself why Jesus would make such a big deal out of looking back? I mean what can happen from just a look, right? Let me give you a quick little Bible history. In Genesis Chapter 3 the woman (Eve) "saw" that the tree was good for food and pleasant to the "eyes."[1] Most have probably heard about Lot's wife, "looking back" when fleeing Sodom and turning into a pillar of salt.[2] But before that happened, her husband Lot first "cast his eyes toward Sodom."[3] Next thing you know, he was pitching his tent toward Sodom.[4] Then a short time later we find him sitting in the gate of Sodom and has his whole family living in the most wicked city on earth.[5] How about King David, who was walking on the rooftop at the time when Kings went to battle. The Scriptures say that David "saw" a woman (ironically named Bathsheba) washing herself and that she was very beautiful to "look upon."[6] How'd all those stories end up? Not so good, huh? Even Peter, who was walking on the water began to sink when he took his eyes off Jesus and started looking around at his surroundings.[7] All of that just from a look.

I mean think about it for a minute. Why is it that commercials for beer, chips, and burgers are always on during all the football games? Do you really think it is a coincidence that supermarkets place certain items at eye level in the store? Or those advertisers spend millions of dollars a year researching packaging and product placement? How about all the home shopping channels and infomercials on TV these days bombarding you with their products, 24/7? It is because the big corporate companies know this simple biblical truth, where your eyes go, your feet will follow.

Here is the thing that none of them, especially the devil, will tell you, it is that you can look but still not see. What I mean by that is that you can look at all the drinking and fun that goes on at a party, but still not see the DUI, your car wrapped around a tree, or you hugging the toilet and promising God that if He will make the room stop spinning that you will never drink again (yeah, I wasn't always saved). You can also look at the naked pictures and pornographic movies that flood our televisions, phones, and computer screens these days, but not see the adulterous affair, the STD, the kids out of wedlock, or the divorce settlement that comes as a result.

Going back to the shopping networks or fast-food commercials for a moment; you can look at all the enticing products and empty calories, but completely miss seeing the crippling debt and depression, or even the diabetes, high blood pressure, and low self-esteem that comes with a lack of self-control and weight of overindulgence. Here is one that will probably hit home with a lot of you; you can look at all the things that you can purchase if you work all that overtime, but definitely not see the effect that you're not being there has on your spouse, kids, and even your relationship with God.

There is a reason that the thing you see Jesus doing most often in the Scriptures is "opening the eyes of the blind" both physically and spiritually. In fact, if you recall Jesus also called the religious leaders of His time "blind guides"[8] among other things, as they looked at Jesus, but couldn't see their Messiah, God, and King standing right in front of them. The thing is, the world will always tell you that seeing is believing, but truth is, God says if you will believe, then you will see.[9] That is why we're told to look not at the things that are seen which are temporary, but to look to the things that are not seen, which are eternal.[10]

> *Two men look out the same prison window,*
> *One sees bars, and the other stars.*
> Anonymous

HOW YOU SEE YOUR LIFE, SHAPES YOUR LIFE

Read the following: IAMNOWHERE! What did you read? Chances are you read either/or:

"I AM NO WHERE!"
"I AM NOW HERE!"

Depending on how you see it, you have either arrived at your destination or are totally lost. Big difference, huh? That really helps illustrate the point I am trying to make. The way you see things in this life goes a long way in determining what you can achieve in this life, and honestly what you will even attempt. I once heard it said that if you think you can or think you can't you're right either way. Just think back on all the times throughout history that people said that something could "NEVER be done!" For example: sail around the globe, climb Mt. Everest, run a mile in under four minutes, split an atom, break the sound barrier, land on the moon, or the thing no one saw being possible: me getting saved, writing a book, and someone putting cheese in the crust of a pizza. (*Smile*)

Seriously, I am sure that those all looked like rock solid, not ever going to happen beliefs at the time, but now we can see that people who were saying never or can't be done, had the wrong focus. All they could see were the failures of the past, rather than the unrealized potential of the future. Same was true with David. Everyone around him said he was too young and too small to go up against Goliath, but while most saw an enemy too big to defeat, David saw a God too big to fail and a giant too big to miss. Instead of focusing on how impossible the challenge ahead of him was, he drew courage by focusing on all that God had already brought him through in his life.[11] That is another good reason why the person who says that it can't be done, should never interfere with the person doing it.

So, I have to ask are you a glass half-empty or glass half-full kind of person? Hopefully after reading this, you're neither as God wants your cup to continuously be running over.[12] Just ask the children of Israel about the overflowing blessings of God. That when God delivered them out of their bondage in Egypt, He brought them forth with gold and silver, none of their clothes wore out, and none were feeble.[13] Or the widow that God blessed through the prophet Elijah, where the little bit of oil that she had never ran out.[14] Or how about the multitude of people that Jesus was able to feed on two separate occasions with just a couple of fish and a few loaves of bread, which also blessed them with leftovers.[15] The sad thing is that many miss what God has for them because they can only see what they don't have, and not see what God does have for them.

From that time many of His disciples
went back and walked with Him no more.
John 6:66 NKJV

NO GOING BACK

Spanish Conquistador Hernando Cortez bravely took his men to Mexico City to march on Montezuma. When they landed at Vera Cruz one of the first things he had them do was to burn, sink, and destroy ALL their ships. He did this so that they wouldn't be tempted to look back, turn back, or go back.

My first question to you is have you sunk all your ships? A ship for you could be an abusive or toxic association, addiction, or activity that is 1- keeping you stuck in the past, or 2- drawing your attention away from the new place that God is trying to take you to, as well as the victory God is trying to give you. Know this, anytime you are tempted to run from where God is directing you to go, the enemy will always have a ship ready for you; just ask Jonah![16]

I am sure I am not the only one to ever have said the words, "I'll never go back to _____ again." (Fill in the blank for yourself, whether it is drinking, gambling, being in debt, jail/prison, that toxic rela-tionship, etc.) Only to find yourself right back there just a short time later. Am I speaking the truth? That is because we spend too much time looking back at and thinking about our past. Even when the only thing that the past is good for is to learn from, not live in. Plus, let's be honest with ourselves, when we look back don't we tend to distort the past? By that I mean that usually we will magnify or remember the good memories and downplay or forget the bad ones. For us guys that is often highlighting the 22 points we scored in that high school bas-ketball game (when in reality was probably more like 12 points), but the whole time failing to remember that the guy you were guarding scored 46 points that same game. Now ladies don't act like you don't do the same thing. I am guessing you probably have some high school sweetheart that you think about every now and again or just wonder how he is doing, right? And I'm also betting that while you remember how cute he was, and what kind of car he drove, you have somehow managed to gloss right over how cheap he was or how he cheated on you with your former friend.

There is a reason why most rearview mirrors on cars warn you that the things you look back at "may appear larger than they actually are." Just as looking back when driving a car can be dangerous, looking back in life can also cause you to crash or to have to turn around because you just drove past the exit you were supposed to take! If you think it can never happen to you as a Christian, then you might want to read 2 Timothy 4:10, where Paul talks about a brother named Demas who forsook him and went back to his worldly living. Or even the Scripture above (John 6:66), where it says that after Jesus challenged them many of His disciples went back and walked with Him no more!

> *Now it came to pass on a certain day, that he went into a ship with his disciples: and he said unto them, Let us go over unto the other side of the lake. And they launched forth. But as they sailed, he fell asleep: and there came down a storm of wind on the lake; and they were filled with water, and were in jeopardy. And they came to him, and awoke him, saying, Master, Master, we perish. Then he arose, and rebuked the wind and the raging of the water: and they ceased, and there was a calm. And he said unto them, Where is your faith?*
> Luke 8:22-25

WHERE'S YOUR FAITH?

Storms can come in many shapes, sizes, and severities. Financial storms, relationship storms, health storms, even legal storms can seemingly arise in a moment and threaten to overwhelm us. The disciples that were with Jesus experienced such a storm and it's interesting that they were so afraid of the weather. First, Jesus the Lord of Lords and King of Kings was in the boat with them. Second, Jesus had clearly told them that they were going to the "other side". He didn't say let's go halfway, and then sink, right? The first thing you need to know is that if Jesus is in your boat and He told you that you will be alright, there really is no need to worry, right? Are you facing a storm? Are you worrying? If so, I have to ask, is Jesus in your boat?

Whatever kind of storm you are facing, or are about to face, great comfort can be found in the first five words of the passage above. It is a good reminder that no matter how bad your storm looks, and no matter how much it feels like it will never end, you can stand confident that the Word of God declares, "Now it came to pass." Even when it came to something as terrible as Jesus being crucified, He wasn't on that cross forever, although, I'm sure those six hours probably felt like an eternity. So, whatever you are facing or going through take comfort in this; it will pass, and you will make it through your storm and get to the other side. The only question that remains is what condition will your house be in after the storm? To answer that, the Bible equates your ability to withstand the storm on your obedience to His Word.[17]

Moving forward what does the passage say that Jesus was doing during the storm? Sleeping, right? I don't know about you, but I've definitely had my fair share of sleepless nights. Tossing, turning, and trying to get my mind to stop thinking about a situation or storm I was going through. Funny thing is I never saw it as an attack of the enemy until the Lord showed me in His Word that when an unclean spirit is gone out of a man, he walks about through dry places seeking rest and finds none.[18] That clearly lets me know that the demonic forces in opposition to God are restless spirits. It makes sense now that Jesus was resting in the boat during the storm, or why He said, "Come unto me, all ye that labour and are heavy laden, and I will give you rest."[19] Not just a good night sleep kind of rest, but He promises rest for our souls.[20] In fact, if you want to know the depth of God's desire to give you rest, look no further than the literal meaning of the first ten names in the genealogy of Jesus. I am talking from *Adam* which means "man" to *Noah* which means "rest". The meaning of the names in order basically says: *Man* is *appointed mortal sorrow*, but the *blessed God shall come down teaching His death shall bring* the *despairing rest*.[21] Is that amazing or what? God's redemptive plan for each of us revealed in the very first book of the Bible!

Now getting back to the passage, what did the disciples do next? They woke up Jesus (the Living Word of God). That is one of the first things each of us needs to do when we are facing a storm, wake up the Word! So, when you are sick, wake up the Word that "By His stripes, we are healed."[22] When you are in trouble, wake up the Word, that He is "an ever-present help in (times of) trouble."[23] When you are broke, wake up the Word that He's the God that, "will meet all your needs."[24] Even when you are under attack, you can wake up the Word so that no weapon that is formed against you will prosper.[25] See when the storm hits you have choices: 1- look around and be distressed, 2- look within and be depressed, or 3- look to Jesus and be at rest.

Lastly, what happened when they woke up Jesus, (the Living Word)? He rose up, spoke to the storm, the storm immediately died down, and they were amazed. See the thing is when Jesus speaks, it is always with authority. He wants us as believers to speak with that same authority. That's why He tells us to say to our mountains "be thou removed, and cast into the sea;" and it shall be done.[26] He also gave us the power to trample on serpents and scorpions, and over ALL the power of the enemy.[27] Isn't it about time that we rest in the Word, wake up the Word, rise up and speak up to our storms and be amazed at what God does? If you don't, you can be sure that your storms are going to speak to you, but it's only when we stop looking back and start living by faith and not by sight that we can have peace in the midst of life's storms. Jesus wants to take you to the other side. Are you ready?

> *But I say unto you, that whosoever looketh on a woman to lust after her hath committed adultery with her already in his heart. And if thy right eye offend thee, pluck it out, and cast it from thee: for it is profitable for thee that one of thy members should perish, and not that thy whole body should be cast into hell.*
> Matthew 5:28-29

PLUCK IT OUT?

After reading this chapter, if you are still not sure that God takes sin and what you look at very seriously, then this verse should eliminate all doubt. Now before you go to the doctor and plead with him to remove your perfectly healthy eye, or even worse play amateur surgeon with your ice cream scooper (sorry for that visual), you should probably know that you can remove both eyes and still be an adulterer or a pervert; as those issues all flow from the heart, which I'll go into more detail in Chapter 12 *Heart Check Time*. The first point the Lord is trying to make here though is to pay attention to what you take in through your eye gates. That is because the light and lamp of the body "is the eye: therefore when thine eye is single, thy whole body is also full of light, but when thine eye is evil, thy body also is full of darkness."[28]

The second point that Jesus is making with this statement is to take sin seriously. The wages of sin is death.[29] Imagine you were to come across a deadly snake like a black mamba. I'll bet you'd get away from it as quick as possible, am I right? That is because we have no doubt about that snake being able to kill us! Unfortunately, many no longer see sin like that. Probably in large part because when we have sinned in the past God didn't strike us down with a lightning bolt or something. So, we just convinced ourselves that it must not have been that big of a deal. Solomon addresses that mindset in Ecclesiastes when he says, "Because sentence against an evil work is not executed speedily, therefore the heart of the sons of men is fully set in them to do evil."[30] But if we ever need a reminder of just how serious God takes sin, you need to look no further than the cross of Christ.

If any of this is speaking to you, or if you have been downplaying some little sin in your life, you should probably read the account of Ananias and Sapphira in Acts Chapter 5. They sold a possession of theirs, kept back part of the money, and then lied about it. Both of them dropped dead from their lie and were dragged out by their feet and buried. And all this was after Jesus' resurrection, so, Christians were already no longer under law, but under grace.[31] We'd be wise to remember the words of the Apostle Paul who wrote, "Shall we continue in sin, that grace may abound? God forbid."[32] God forbid indeed! While I am sure most of us would probably say that lying isn't the worst thing we've heard of or even done this week, it's a stark reminder that God's ways not our ways. More importantly, God takes sin very seriously. So, when Jesus says to pluck it out or cut if off, what He is really saying is take sin seriously and remove anything or remove yourself from anything that is going to cause you to sin. That way you don't miss out on the abundant and eternal life that God has for you.

What is it that you are looking at/focusing on: your problems or God's promises?

Are you able to rest in your storms like Jesus, or are you worried like the disciples?

Is there anything in your life that you have told yourself you can never accomplish? If that is the case, what does God say about it?

Has there been a time in your life when just a look led to some unforeseen consequences? Commit to examining what you are looking at now that could have a similar negative outcome.

Is looking back on past hurts, failures, or disappointments hindering you from reaching your full potential? If so, what can you do differently? (Confess it to God, draw encouragement from God's Word, shift your focus to things God has gotten you through or helped you overcome in the past, etc.)

CHAPTER 6

FIGHT THE GOOD FIGHT (IDENTIFYING OUR ENEMY)

*Fight the good fight of faith; take
hold of the eternal life to which you were
called, and you made the good confession in
the presence of many witnesses.*
1 Timothy 6:12 NASB

You may not realize it, but you are at war. I am not talking about the war on drugs or the war on crime and terrorism. I am not even talking about the war on cholesterol, which by the way many of us are losing. No. The war that I am talking about is the war for the souls of every person on the planet. Got your attention now? I thought so.

As in any war, you need to know exactly who it is that you are fighting. Their tactics, strengths, weaknesses, allies, weapons, and objectives. But you will also need to know your own strengths, weaknesses, allies, and the weapons that are at your disposal. That way you can begin to successfully come up with a plan to achieve victory. Makes sense, right?

You should know up front that your enemy isn't playing. He desires to kill you,[1] and will use ANY and ALL means at his disposal to achieve that goal, but if he can't kill you, he wants to take you captive. And if he cannot do either of those, then he wants to take away your ability or even desire to fight. Yeah, it is that serious. So, if you genuinely want to experience the miraculous power of God in your life, live up to your God-given potential, and take hold of the eternal life to which you were called, then you are going to have to fight, and fight hard, the good fight of faith.

IDENTIFYING OUR ENEMY

> *For we wrestle not against flesh and blood, but*
> *against principalities, against powers, against*
> *the rulers of darkness of this world, against*
> *spiritual wickedness in high places.*
> Ephesians 6:12

Let me ask you something, when you hear the word "enemy" who comes to mind? Your ex, your in-laws, that nosy neighbor, a former bully, or maybe those mean girls from work or school? How about the IRS, that super critical (hypocritical) couple at church, or that know-it-all supervisor who just so happens to be related to the boss? Maybe you think your enemy is Russia, or that crazy little North Korean dictator. If you grew up in the 60's or 70's then your enemy was probably "the man". Here's the thing, while your enemy may work through any or all of those agencies or individuals, none of them are you real enemy. How do I know? Because we wrestle not against flesh and blood.

Now you would think it would be easy to identify who it is you are fighting, but you would be wrong. Unlike in the movies where the enemy soldiers wear clearly marked uniforms and bad guys wear black hats, that's just not the case with our enemy. We really shouldn't be surprised though. If you were to ask someone that fought in Vietnam, Iraq, or Afghanistan I am sure they'd tell you that one of the most critical and challenging aspects in any war or conflict is identifying exactly who it is you're fighting. So, I won't leave you in suspense any longer. If you don't already know, your enemy is the world, the flesh, and the devil.

THE WORLD

> *Ye adulterers and adulteresses, know ye not that*
> *the friendship of the world is enmity with God?*
> *Whosoever therefore will be a friend of the*
> *world is the enemy of God.*
> James 4:4

You are probably saying, how can the world be my enemy when we all live in the world? Let me explain. The word *world* that I am talking about is from the Greek word *kosmos*,[2] which means the orderly arrangement/unbelieving system which Satan has orchestrated in opposition to God. Let me illustrate a couple of ways that the world's system (kosmos) is against you. The jails and prisons need you to commit crimes and violate the conditions of your probation and parole so they can build, fund, and staff correctional complexes around the globe. By the way, while it may not be happening in large numbers yet in this country, a lot of those worldly correctional systems are being used to persecute, torture, and even kill Christians. Many for just professing their faith in Christ or for sharing the good news of the Gospel, but if you know anything about history then you know that there is nothing new under the sun.

The banks and various credit agencies need you to be broke or in a hurry to purchase something so you will borrow money from them; often at outrageous rates of interest. Truth be told, if at some point you are late or even unable to make your payments that is alright with them as well. Then they can hit you with some late fees, penalties, or just repo your house, car, or jewelry. The bar association needs you to be hurt, wronged, maimed, killed, or just angry and unforgiving towards someone so they can charge you $140+ an hour to try and give you what only God can give you, peace of mind and justice. And lastly, the pharmaceutical companies (pharmaceutical comes from Greek word *pharmakeia*,[3] which means sorcery, spells, drugs, occult powers, witchcraft) need you to have some disease or aliment so they can charge you some astronomical amount for their new drug. Which, by the way, will probably require you to take two to three other pills for the side effects from the first drug.

Those are just a few of the ways that the world and its system are against you. No wonder why Satan is referred to as "the god (little g) of this world"[4] and he has blinded the minds of them that believe not. That is why we are told to not be conformed to this world,[5] and to be in the world and not of the world.[6] Also to love not the world, nor the things in the world,[7] and to keep ourselves unspotted from the world. With that being said, you should pause for a moment and take a serious look at what you love, think about, pursue, and live like? If it's the world, you need to know that the whole world lies in wickedness[8] and the world is passing away,[9] but the good news is that through the cross of Christ the world is crucified to us and us to the world.[10]

THE FLESH

For the flesh lusts against the Spirit,
and the Spirit against the flesh; and these
are contrary to one another, so that you do
not do the things that you wish.
Galatians 5:17 NKJV

If you struggled with the world being your enemy, then this section is probably going to be just as challenging. There was a man in Alaska that bred some of the toughest dogs in the world. Unfortunately, he often pitted them against one another for sport. What made him so famous was his seemingly uncanny ability to pick the winning dog every time. Finally, someone got him to share his secret for success. He said, "Its simple, the one I feed the day before ALWAYS wins!" I tell you that because the same is true of us. You are a Spirit that lives in a body, and that has an eternal soul. If you sow (plant, spread, feed) to the flesh (and when I say flesh I am talking about your sinful, carnal nature that is in opposition to the will of God), you shall of the flesh reap destruction.

But if you sow (plant, spread, feed) your Spirit, you shall of the Spirit reap eternal life.[11]

The commercials will tell you a Snickers candy bar satisfies, but if that were true, why do you usually want another one an hour later? Or if you are like me, five minutes later. Ever try and eat just one potato chip or french fry? How about one doughnut or piece of chocolate? Maybe your "just can't stop at one" is a cigarette, cup of coffee, or shot of alcohol? Even if none of the things I listed above move you, I'll bet there is something you have a hard time saying no to, right? Maybe it is clothes, cars, jewelry, shoes, games, or gadgets. That is because the flesh is never satisfied, but you don't have to take my word for it. King Solomon, who is widely regarded as one of the richest, wisest kings ever states that, "All the labour of man is for his mouth, and yet the appetite is not filled."[12] He later went on to say that all his power, possessions, wisdom, and even women (he had 700 wives and 300 concubines[13]) at the end of the day were all vanity and vexation of spirit,[14] basically meaningless.

If you are still not convinced that there is a real war raging with the flesh, listen to the words of the Apostle Paul, who God used to pen almost half of the books in the New Testament, "For I know that in me (that is, in the flesh,) dwelleth no good thing: for to will is present with me; but how to perform that which is good I find not. For the good that I would I do not: but the evil which I would not, that I do."[15] That is because the Spirit is willing, but the flesh is weak.[16] No wonder the Scripture not only tells us to have no confidence in the flesh,[17] but that cursed is the person who trusts in the arm of flesh.[18]

So, who is currently and consistently winning the battle in your life? Is it the works of the flesh which are: immorality, impurity, sensuality, idolatry, sorcery, enmities, strife, jealousy, outbursts of anger, disputes, dissensions, factions, envying, drunkenness, and carousing?[19] Or is it the fruits of the Spirit which are love, joy, peace, patience, kindness, goodness, faithfulness, gentleness, and self-control?[20]

THE DEVIL

> *And the great dragon was cast out, that*
> *old serpent, called the Devil, and Satan, which*
> *deceiveth the whole world: he was cast out into*
> *the earth, and his angels were cast out with him.*
> Revelation 12:9

The devil is a fitting name for our enemy, and not just because it has "evil" in it. But he has many names: Adversary,[21] Ancient Serpent,[22] Accuser of the brethren,[23] *Apollyon*- destroyer,[24] Lucifer,[25] Satan,[26] *Belial*- worthless one,[27] and *Beelzebub*- dung god.[28] That last one literally means *lord of the flies*. This seems to me the most fitting, as wherever there is something dead, stinking, or rotten you will find him there. He is a thief and a murderer[29] and while he doesn't have weapons of mass destruction, he does have weapons of mass deception. That's because he is the father of lies.[30] In fact his biggest lie is to get people to believe that he's been misjudged, or even more so that he doesn't really exist. If you have a picture of some ugly, red, scaly creature with horns and a pitchfork you should rethink that. The Scripture describes him before his fall as the anointed cherub that had every precious stone as his covering.[31] It also says that he was perfect in all his ways until iniquity was found in him and that his heart was lifted up because of his beauty.[32] In fact if you think that he'd be easy to identify you may want to read 2 Corinthians 11:14-15, where it says that Satan masquerades himself as an angel of light.

As I mentioned in the intro, the devil is a fallen angel, not a fallen God. That means he is not God's equal. Despite his many lies to the contrary, he is not *omnipotent*- all powerful, *omnipresent*- all present; everywhere, and he is definitely not *omniscient*- all knowing. The book of Job confirms all this as Satan presented himself to God, basically had to ask God's permission to attack and afflict Job, and was dead wrong about proclaiming that Job would curse God for all he'd been through.[33] He is also a defeated foe, destined for the lake of fire,[34] but that doesn't mean we can take him lightly, as even a venomous snake with its head cut off can still administer a lethal bite if you're not careful around it. Well, I think we have spent enough time talking about our enemy, don't you? He has tormented and terrorized me and my family for way too long. You too, huh? So, let's use the rest of this chapter to take a look at all the amazing things God has blessed us with so that we can walk in victory over that sucker! Amen!!

YOUR ARMOR

*Put on the full armor of God, so that you
will be able to stand firm against the schemes
of the devil. Stand firm therefore, having
girded your loins with truth, and having put on the
breastplate of righteousness, and having shod
your feet with the preparation of the Gospel of
peace, in addition to all, taking up the shield of
faith with which you will be able to extinguish
all the flaming arrows of the evil one. And take the*

helmet of salvation, and the sword of the Spirit,
which is the word of God. With all prayer and
petition pray at all times in the Spirit, and with
this in view, be on alert with all perseverance
and petition for all the saints.
Ephesians 6:11, 14-18 NASB1995

I have a buddy that was in the army back when Saddam Hussein was shooting missiles at Kuwait. At the time it was feared that Saddam was putting chemicals in the missiles so the United States got involved and was using its Scud missiles to help shoot down Saddam's missiles. Because of the possible threat of chemicals being used, an alarm would sound every time a missile was fired, and everyone would then have to put on their chemical suits. My friend said that after a couple weeks of the alarm sounding at all hours of the night and early morning, people in his squad started getting complacent and didn't always put on their suits. They just assumed that it was another false alarm being sounded like all the other times. Sadly, during one of those disregarded alarms, chemicals were actually deployed, and my friend came back with some permanent damage to his skin and lungs.

I say all this to say, are you taking the alarms that God is sounding seriously? If so, are you putting your armor on? Every day? Maybe you aren't even aware of the incredible armor that God has prepared and provided for you? In either case, let's take a closer look at the armor, and exactly what it's for.

BELT OF TRUTH

Can I tell you the truth, the whole truth, and nothing but the truth, so help me God? Can you handle the truth? Are you sure? Reason I ask is because truth is heavy, which is why few ever attempt to carry it.[35] With the devil being the father of all lies, it should not come as a big surprise that the first piece of God's armor is a belt of truth. It is also important to note that the belt holds all the armor together and girds our loins or our reproductive organs, which is because nothing good or true can ever be birthed from a lie. Especially not the new, abundant, born again, fruitful life that God wants to birth in and through you. In order to effectively wear this crucial piece of God's armor, you are first going to have to recognize and repent of every lie of the enemy that you have mixed and mistaken for the truth. That way you can not only know the truth and speak the truth, but develop a lifestyle rooted and grounded in truth.

BREASTPLATE OF RIGHTEOUSNESS

I'm sure I don't need to tell you how important the breastplate is for a soldier. It helps protect not only your heart, but many other vital organs as well. The key to remember is that it is a breastplate of "righteousness," which as we've already established is symbolic of right standing with God, and only comes by faith in the shed blood of Jesus for the remission of our sins.[36] As the Scriptures declare, ALL our attempts at righteousness are as "filthy rags"[37] so you definitely want to make sure you not only put on the breastplate, but put on the right one! I don't know about you, but I'd hate to go into battle with something guarding my heart that was filthy, faulty, or flimsy!

FEET SHOD WITH THE PREPEARATION OF THE GOSPEL OF PEACE

Do you have peace in your life? Peace does not mean the absence of pain, persecution, or problems, but it does mean having the presence of God during all that stuff. Jesus confirmed this when He said, "In me you may have peace, but in the world you shall have tribulation.[38] Jesus is the "Prince of Peace."[39] Peace is a fruit of the Spirit.[40] The Hebrew word for peace is *Shalom*,[41] which is often used as a greeting or in conjunction with a blessing in Jewish culture. It also means tranquility, prosperity, favor, health, and safety. When Jesus sent His disciples out, He told them if the household received them to let their peace come upon it. If not, to shake off the dust from their feet and keep moving.[42] The Scriptures also say "How lovely on the mountains Are the feet of him who brings good news, Who announces peace And brings good news of happiness, Who announces salvation, And says to Zion, 'Your God Reigns!'"[43] Do you realize that we all have the awesome privilege and responsibility to bring the good news of the gospel to those in desperate need of that news? I won't lie to you; it's a dangerous assignment in enemy territory, but countless individuals will perish without this news. Are your feet shod with the preparation of the Gospel of Peace? If not, what is hindering you from lacing up and getting in the fight?

SHIELD OF FAITH

I can remember when the U.S. was talking about creating a missile defense shield. I am pretty sure they called it *Star Wars*. Had they simply read God's Word they could have saved a ton of time (and money) as they would have realized that while we do need a shield to extinguish the flaming missiles the enemy shoots our way, it is a SHIELD OF FAITH! While your enemy may come against your health, household, and happiness and he may even attack your finances, freedom, and family, he is really only after one thing, YOUR FAITH! You are probably asking why my faith? It's because we walk by faith,[44] live by faith,[45] receive healing by faith,[46] move mountains with faith (the size of a mustard seed),[47] and even are saved by grace through faith.[48] In addition, you'll need faith if you want to extinguish all the flaming missiles of the enemy. But more than anything, the devil knows that without faith it is impossible to please God.[49]

HELMET OF SALVATION

I see so many kids these days being filmed doing super risky tricks on ramps, roads, and rails. They all have one thing in common, no helmets. While not wearing a helmet may be cool in a secular world, it is crazy in spiritual warfare. An often overlooked, but effective part of any battle is propaganda. It is where the enemy tries to get into their opponent's head before, or even during the battle to distract, defeat, or just discourage them from fighting any more, or at all. This tactic was used extensively by both sides in World Wars 1 and 2, as well as in the Vietnam War. Another good example of someone using this technique in battle was Goliath. Just as intimidating as his size was what he said to the Israelite army. The Scripture says that his bold defiance and brash threats caused King Saul and all Israel to be dismayed and greatly afraid.[50] There is a reason why our adversary is described as a "roaring lion."[51] The lion's roar is designed to get its prey to fear, freeze, or react foolishly, thereby ensuring the lion a victory. That is why we desperately need to put on our helmets of salvation, to not only keep the devil from hitting us upside our heads, but even more importantly from getting inside our heads with his lies.

In closing this section, you may have noticed I left off a couple components of the armor, specifically the Sword of the Spirit and praying in the Spirit. That is because they fit better in the next section of what God has blessed us with in this epic battle.

OUR WEAPONS

For though we walk in the flesh, we
do not war after the flesh: (For the weapons of
our warfare are not carnal, but mighty through
God to the pulling down of strong holds;) Casting
down imaginations, and every high thing that

exalteth itself against the knowledge of God, and
bringing into captivity every thought to the
obedience of Christ.
2 Corinthians 10:3-5

This is hard for me to admit as a father and a man, but my youngest son Cory dominates me at video games, especially ones involving head-to-head competition. Seems like the only one I can hold my own at is the old school Mario Karts, largely because I know how to drop a banana peel or throw a cabbage. The advantage that allows my son to crush me at all those games is simple, he knows, is familiar, and proficient with all the weapons.

The world will tell you that what you don't know won't hurt you, but that makes absolutely no sense in the natural or the spiritual. Let me ask you, would not knowing that you had cancer hurt you? What if the brakes on your car were about to go out, wouldn't that be something that you would want to know? And, I would hope that after reading this chapter you realize that NOT knowing you are in a war or NOT knowing that you have a real enemy that is trying to kill, steal or destroy you and your family,[52] can not only be hurtful, but catastrophic.

So now for the real question, do you know your weapons? Even more importantly, how to use them? For the record our weapons are: The Word of God,[53] the name of Jesus,[54] faith in God,[55] submission to God,[56] the cross of Christ,[57] the blood of the Lamb (Jesus), the word of our testimony, and loving not our lives unto death,[58] prayer and fasting,[59] and praise,[60] to name a few.

I know that many, maybe even all of the weapons I've listed above may be unfamiliar to some of you reading this. But rest assured that they are ALL powerful and battle tested! Looking at the weapons, I am sure the one you are probably wondering about the most is praise, right? You are probably asking how can praise be a weapon against our enemy? Another good question, glad you asked. In the Old Testament when an overwhelming multitude of Moabites, Ammonites, and Edomites came against Judah[61] (by the way, *Judah* literally means praise)[62] Jehoshaphat, King of Judah, appointed singers and worshippers to go out before the army and praise the Lord.[63] If you thought that Spartan soldiers from the movie "300" were bold and courageous, imagine being faced with a seemingly overwhelming adversary and sending the worship team out to lead the battle. The incredible part is that it worked! Through that act of obedience, the Lord set ambushes, and the praise so confused the enemy that they ended up destroying themselves.[64] It is easy to praise God after the victory, but how about praising Him going into the battle? It's easy when you know the following: 1- the battle belongs to the Lord[65] 2- God inhabits the praises of His people[66] 3- God has already given us the ultimate victory through Jesus Christ our Lord[67] and 4- the best reason of all, we serve a God who is worthy of ALL our praise![68]

Before I move on to the next chapter, I want to share a little story with you to help illustrate another tactic of the enemy. There was a man that had a farm in an extremely remote area. Every morning, the farmer would take his best horse out to plow his field. Six days a week, from sunrise to sunset, the man and his horse would work tirelessly, tilling the soil. One day after a hard day of plowing, it was getting dark when the man began his walk back home. About halfway there, his horse suddenly fell into a dried up, abandoned well, that someone had placed a thin piece of plywood over. The man was distraught at the loss of his faithful horse and companion. The farmer lacked the money, manpower, and machinery to retrieve the body of his beloved horse, so he decided that the respectful thing to do, as well as to ensure that this never happened again was to fill in the old, dried up well with dirt.

The man toiled all night long dumping wheelbarrow after wheelbarrow full of dirt into the well. As the sun began to rise, the man dumped what felt like his 1,000th load of dirt into the abandoned well. Much to his surprise he looked and saw his trusty horse now standing only a few feet from the top of the well. It soon became apparent to the man that the horse had shaken off the very thing that was meant to bury it and put it under its feet.

This is a powerful visual of what God has given us the ability to do when it comes to our enemy. The Scripture declares that in Christ we have the power to tread on serpents and scorpions.[69] It also tells us that "the God of peace shall bruise Satan under your feet shortly."[70] This is why Joseph was able to boldly declare that what others meant for evil, God meant for good.[71] It is also how the Apostle Paul was able to shake off a deadly viper that latched on his hand when he was shipwrecked on the Isle of Malita.[72]

I really hope that what I have written here has opened your eyes to not only the tactics of your enemy, but the very real war that is waging around you for your eternal soul. I would be remiss in my duty as a Christian if I didn't warn you that this knowledge comes at a price. After reading all this, it is probably going to seem like you are under attack like never before and maybe that will be the case because the time I spent writing and researching for this book, I was under physical and spiritual attack like I have never experienced before! More importantly is the fact that you are now just more aware of the attack that has been there the whole time.

In either case, take comfort in the knowledge that while weapons will be formed against you, God declares they won't prosper.[73] The enemy may come in like a flood, but the Spirit of the Lord promises to lift up a standard against him.[74] The devil may knock you down, but he can't keep you down. He may occasionally beat you, but in Christ he can never defeat you! So next time he tries to throw dirt on you, don't just lie there, rise up, shake him off, and put him under your feet where he belongs. In order to do that you are going to have to fight, and fight with all you have got... that good fight of faith!

Are you sick and tired of the enemy wreaking havoc in the lives of you and your family?

If the answer to that is yes, after reading this, have you been fighting the good fight? And more importantly, have you been fighting your real enemy?

PERSONALLY APPLYING CENTRAL TRUTH

Will you commit to putting on the whole armor of God every morning?

The Word of God not only builds your faith, but is a powerful weapon. Make a plan to read the Bible at least once a day for the next 12 months and memorize at least a Scripture a week. That way by this time next year you will be better prepared for battle.

CHAPTER 7

EVEN NOW
(ROLL BACK THE STONE)

Life is 10% what happens to you
and 90% how you react to it.
Charles R. Swindoll

D
o you know anyone that has one of those perfectly kept, show-room quality living rooms? I know that is a super old school thing, so if you do know someone likely it is a grandma or great aunt. Growing up that person for me was my mom. She had the living room to top all living rooms. Truthfully it should have been called the "off limits" or "no living in here" room. I am talking carpet that had been cleaned so many times you could see the grooves from the wheels of the vacuum cleaner. It also had a couple of those lamps with the stained glass lampshades, sitting on perfectly placed white lace doylies. Oh yeah, and how could I forget to mention the couch with the plastic on it, which made no sense at all, as no one in our family was ever allowed to sit on the living room couch in the first place. Starting to get the picture? We are talking a hospital clean, museum exhibit worthy living room. With my mom this mania extended out to the guest bathroom as well, which I found out the hard way one day as a kid when yep, I did the unthinkable; I actually washed and dried my hands in the guest bathroom! Problem was I used the flower shaped, scented Avon soap, and dried my hands with one of the perfectly placed decorative hand towels, which unbeknownst to me were intricately, hand

crocheted by my grandmother. Needless to say, I didn't make that mistake again, as I wasn't able to sit down for a week. (Sorry, I know spanking isn't politically correct these days.)

Point being, my mom, like a lot of people, was greatly concerned about outward appearances and what other people thought. I say all that because even though you likely don't have a meticulously kept living room like my mom, I'm betting that there are probably more than a few of you reading this that are working hard to keep up your own outward façade. But instead of with a living room, it is with your life. To the casual observer, I am sure you look like you have got everything all together and are doing great, but what would people see if they were to pull back the curtain and look at some of the proverbial "other rooms" that you really don't want anyone to see? Like your kitchen (what you eat and take in), your recreation room (what entertains you), your bedroom (what you are intimate with), your closet (what you put on), and your attic/basement (what you have hid or do not want to let go of). All of which leads me to ask the question, is the you that people get to see healthier than the you that they don't get to see? If the answer is yes, then who are you really fooling? See we all go through stuff in life, and without a doubt some of it is going to be terrible, hurtful, or embarrassing. Thing is you can choose to spend a lot of time, energy, and even money to try and make it seem like everything is just fine, but at the end of the day, what is the point of that? All you end up doing is keeping yourself from ever getting prayer, encouragement, or even help for what you are struggling with or going through.

I don't know how much of the Bible you have read. Maybe you don't even own a Bible, or your Bible has been on the shelf so long it is covered in dust. In either case you should know that it is full of incredible, real life testimonies, transformations, tragedies, and even numerous timeless truths that we can apply to our day-to-day situations, struggles, and even sicknesses. In this chapter we are going to look at how a particular family dealt with their own faith, frustration, sickness, sorrow, doubt, disappointment, and even death. Things we all have or eventually will have to deal with. Amen?

LAZARUS IS SICK

> *Now a certain man was sick, named Lazarus,*
> *of Bethany, the town of Mary and her sister*
> *Martha. (It was that Mary which anointed the*
> *Lord with ointment, and wiped his feet with her*
> *hair, whose brother Lazarus was sick). Therefore,*
> *his sisters sent unto him, saying, Lord, behold,*
> *he whom thou lovest is sick. When Jesus heard*
> *that, he said, This sickness is not unto death, but*
> *for the glory of God, that the Son of God might*
> *be glorified thereby. Now Jesus loved Martha,*
> *and her sister, and Lazarus. When he had heard*
> *therefore that he was sick, he abode two days*
> *still in the same place where he was.*
> John 11:1-6

There is a whole lot going on in just these first six verses. Lazarus and his two sisters, Mary and Martha, lived in Bethany, a small town located on the eastern slope of the Mount of Olives. This is about two miles to the east of Jerusalem. Jesus loved Martha, Mary, and Lazarus, and they knew, loved, and had a personal relationship with Him. In fact, Scripture indicates that Jesus would spend time at their home from time to time. To the casual observer, everything looks great, right? Yet in the midst of all that, we read that Lazarus is sick. Now you would think that loving Jesus, Him loving you, being in a relationship with Him, and even having Jesus at your house from time to time would keep you from getting sick? Maybe the fact that they only entertained Jesus from "time to time" is why Lazarus got sick in the first place. Either way, the love is real, the relationship with Jesus is real, but still there is sickness.

Now there are all kinds of sicknesses. Carsick, lovesick, seasick, dope sick, and plain old illness and disease sick. While we don't know what the specific kind of sickness that Lazarus was suffering from was, it was obviously serious enough that his sisters urgently sent word to Jesus. Isn't this pretty much a microcosm of the church today? By that I mean that other than the Pastor, a few older men, and some kids most of our congregations are a bunch of faithful women reaching out to Jesus for their sick brothers in the church?

Before I start to really unpack this situation, someone may want to let the church know that you can love Jesus, have Jesus love you, be in a relationship with Jesus, even have Him at your house from time to time, and still get sick or struggle. There seems to be a judgmental, religious mindset these days with some church goers that if you get sick or struggle then you must have some secret sin, lack of faith, or just not really be saved. Sad but true mentality, huh? Nothing new under the sun though, as even the disciples of Jesus voiced that mentality when they came across a man born blind. They asked Jesus who sinned, the man or his parents that he was born blind? Jesus answered, "Neither hath this man sinned, nor his parents: but that the works of God should be manifest in him."[1] This judgmental spirit could be the reason that todays "sick Lazarus" avoid going to church or just sit there and suffer in silence.

The Scriptures do not specifically say it, but maybe it was that fear of being judged or looked down on that kept Lazarus from calling out to Jesus himself. Or perhaps it was some of that mentality that men are taught at an early age that men never ask for help or show any weakness that we exposed earlier in Chapter 4 *Grow Up Already, Would You? (I'll Never Be Like My Parents)*. Whatever the reason, Lazarus, like many of us, can be grateful for godly sisters that reached out to Jesus for him in his time of need. Before we move forward, in this biblical account it is also worth noting that when Jesus heard the news about his friend's health, rather than heading to Bethany as quickly as possible, Jesus chose to stay right where He was for two more days. This is a prime example that Jesus doesn't always move when we say, think, want, or expect Him to, but rather when God the Father says to move.[2]

EVEN NOW

Then said Martha unto Jesus, Lord, if
thou hadst been here, my brother had not died.
But I know, that even now, whatsoever thou wilt
ask of God, God will give it thee.
John 11:21-22

Lazarus isn't sick anymore, now HE'S DEAD! Ever been upset with God when something didn't turn out like you thought it would or prayed for it to? Be honest now, I think it's safe to say we've probably all experienced that at one time or another. I say that because we can hear some of that in Lazarus' sister, Martha's words. Let's be honest for a moment, like Martha we are not always real happy with Jesus when we think that He is late or should have prevented something from happening. But before you raise your voice or shake your fist toward Heaven you should know that there is big difference between God allowing something, and God causing something. You can rest assured that if Almighty God is allowing something to happen, then it is for your good,[3] for your growth,[4] or for His glory;[5] most times all three. You should also know that there will be times when God lets things go from improbable to impossible, from hard to hopeless, even from bad to worse before they get better. That way you will know for sure that it was God that turned things around.

I still remember being really angry with God when my mom passed away in '96. Especially when two years prior she got diagnosed with ALS, a vicious disease that attacks your nervous system. Basically, it breaks down a person's body, while leaving their mind intact. So having to watch my once vibrant, kindhearted, mother lose motor function and even the ability to speak, was beyond hard, but my anger with God was short lived as God comforted me[6] and gave me the strength to encourage my mom, even during the worst of it. He also revealed to me that He paints on an eternal canvas so big that I can't comprehend it. Plus all those things that currently make no sense, seem unfair or wrong in this life all get set straight in eternity.

I don't know what it is you're facing or struggling with. Maybe it is sickness or separation from someone you love. Maybe you have a failing business or impending bankruptcy. Maybe you are facing a career change or criminal charge. Perhaps it is an untimely divorce decree, unexpected doctor's diagnosis, depression or even death. Whatever it is though that you are facing, you need to know that we have a universe creating,[7] body healing,[8] dead rising,[9] water walking,[10] mountain moving,[11] prison door opening,[12] miracle working,[13] **EVEN NOW GOD!**

So, if your marriage or health is failing; if your car loan, credit card, or parole got denied; if you have lost your job or lost contact with your kids; or even if the bank says you only have a couple weeks to pay or the doctor says you only have a couple weeks to live, you need to know that God is I Am,[14] not I was or I will be. Which simply put means He is not just an even now, but a RIGHT NOW God. You don't have to take my word for it, just look at Abraham, Joseph, Daniel, Jonah, and the three Hebrew boys. Each one faced a seemingly insurmountable situation. Abraham was told by God that he would be the father of many nations,[15] yet 24 years later he was 99 years old, and his wife was 90 years old and still nothing.[16] Joseph was shown in a dream the amazing future God had for him but was then thrown in a pit,[17] sold into slavery[18] (both by his brothers), and later was even cast into prison for a sex offense that he didn't commit.[19] Daniel was thrown into a lion's den, just for praying to God.[20] Jonah was cast into the sea and swallowed up by a great fish.[21] Let us not forget about the three Hebrew boys Shadrach, Meshach, and Abednego who were thrown into a fiery furnace that was heated seven times hotter than normal but walked out unscathed.[22] In the midst of all that, each had their own "even now" moment with God, and wouldn't you know it, God blessed, delivered, showed up, and kept His word each time. If God did it for them, He'll do it for you! For with God there is no respect of persons.[23] Now let's get back to Lazarus and see what else we can learn from this incredible biblical account.

JESUS WEPT

> *Then when Mary was come where Jesus was,*
> *and saw him, she fell down at his feet, saying unto*
> *him, Lord, if you hadst been here, my brother had*
> *not died. When Jesus therefore saw her weeping,*
> *and the Jews also weeping which came with her,*
> *he groaned in the Spirit, and was troubled.*
> *And said, Where have ye laid him? They said unto*
> *him, Lord, come and see. Jesus wept. Then said*
> *the Jews, Behold how he loved him! And some*
> *of them said, Could not this man, which opened*
> *the eyes of the blind, have caused that even this*
> *man should not have died? Jesus therefore again*
> *groaning in himself cometh to the grave. It was a*
> *cave, and a stone lay upon it.*
> John 11:32-38

Now we not only have Martha's sister Mary criticizing the Lord's timing and questioning his love for Lazarus, but the Jewish church folk as well. That is pretty ironic, as throughout His time on earth the religious leaders were constantly attacking Jesus for the miraculous things that he did do.[24] Now they have the nerve to bad mouth Him for what they thought He should have, would have, or could have done. Just thought I would point that out before we move on.

Jesus wept. Not only is this an easy verse to memorize, but an extremely powerful visual to consider. Ever asked yourself why Jesus wept? I mean, I know why I weep; either I'm sad, hurting, or just fearful about how things are going to turn out, but this is Jesus and He knew that He was going to raise Lazarus from the dead. Remember in John 11:4 (above), He said "This sickness is not unto death, but for the glory of God." So why the tears? First you should know that there is an amazing principle throughout the Scriptures of the *Goel* or Kinsman Redeemer.[25] It is basically where you had to be a relative or near relative in order to redeem something or someone. The Kinsman redemption had a couple of key elements. First, it was of persons or of an inheritance,[26] second, the redeemer must be able to redeem,[27] and finally, the redemption is completed by the Kinsman Redeemer paying the just demand in full.[28] In fact, when someone owed a debt, they would often write the debt on an animal skin and nail it to a wooden post. Then a kinsman would cover or cross out the debt.[29] What a beautiful picture of Christ and His bride, the church. So, if you had any questions on why God had to send His Son to be born into the world in the flesh to die for our sins, it is because He had to be kin to us to be our Kinsman Redeemer and purchase us back from the bondage of sin and death.

Getting back to the tears... isn't it comforting to know that we have a God that can not only sympathize with all that we go through,[30] but loves each of us so much that He rejoices when we rejoice, and mourns when we mourn.[31] That is good news, amen?

TAKE AWAY THE STONE

Jesus said, Take ye away the stone.
Martha, the sister of him that was dead,
saith unto him, Lord, by this time he stinketh:
for he hath been dead four days.
John 11:39

What do we do when we give up on something? We roll a stone in front of it. There are some stones that God rolls back, like at the tomb of Jesus,[32] Then there are others that Jesus comes along and says for us to take Him to the place that we gave up, lost hope, or stopped believing what He said about the situation, and He asks us to roll back the stone. Let's get real, just like Martha there are some things that we are embarrassed to open up and have Jesus take a look at what's really behind there, am I right? Especially when it has been there for a while, and it stinks.

So, what have you given up on and tried to hide or bury? Is it your marriage, career, or having a better relationship with your kids? Maybe it is getting in better shape, owning a home, or being stronger in your faith? Whatever it is, if you really want to see the miraculous power of God at work, you are going to have to take Jesus there and **roll back the stone!** I tell you this as it really is our secrets that keep us sick and keep us from living the abundant life that God has promised us.

LAZARUS COME FORTH

And when He thus had spoken,
he cried with a loud voice, Lazarus come forth.
And he that was dead came forth, bound
hand and foot with graveclothes: and his face
was bound about with a napkin. Jesus saith unto
them, Loose him, and let him go.
John 11:43-44

It's a good thing that Jesus called Lazarus by name, otherwise all the tombs would have emptied out completely. Perhaps you are trying to figure out why God chose to raise up Lazarus this way? I used to wonder the same thing; then one day the Lord revealed to me that this miracle was basically the last straw for the Jewish religious leaders. From that day forward they took counsel to put Jesus to death,[33] which we now know was necessary for us to be redeemed from the curse of sin and death.[34] Just another example of God painting on an eternal canvas that we cannot comprehend.

Here is the last point I want to make; God can call you out of a dead place, but you are still going to need some help getting loose. I don't know what God has or is currently calling you out of? It could be drugs, debt, or depression? Loneliness or lying? Gangs or gambling? Anger or alcohol? Pain, poverty, or pornography? Maybe it is even unbelief or an unforgiving spirit? Whatever it is, you need to know that Jesus not only wants to save you,[35] but set you free.[36] There is a reason that those who are still alive do not feel comfortable in a graveyard, it is because you don't belong there. If you are ever going to reach your full God-given potential, then you are going to need some help getting loose from those old slave and grave clothes.

When it comes to your "dead place", you may have to leap out, run out, crawl out, or even cry out, but like Lazarus, God is calling many of you out today. **Will you come?**

If so, will you pray this prayer with me:

> *Heavenly Father,*
>
> *I thank You for calling me out of darkness and into Your glorious light. Lord, You have given me the victory; help me to walk in it. Create in me a clean heart oh God and renew a right spirit within me. Help me to lay aside every weight, sin, struggle, and sickness that I have tried to hide or bury; as well as, to roll back every stone that I put in front of my secret doubt or disappointment.*
>
> *I ask all this in Jesus name, Amen!*

Do you see yourself in the account of Lazarus, Mary, and Martha?

Is there anything that you believed God for, but it only got worse, not better? If so, are you holding on to any resentment towards God because of it?

Is there any area of your life, like your marriage, finances, health, or even your faith, that you are trying to keep up the appearance that everything is good, when it is not? If so, will you reach out to a Pastor or strong brother or sister in the Lord for prayer, godly counsel, and assistance?

CHAPTER 8

OBSTACLES
(DO YOU WANT TO BE MADE WHOLE?)

With every opportunity comes an obstacle,
and with every obstacle comes an opportunity.
Anonymous

Growing up, I always had dirt bikes and my sister always had animals and pets. She had a hamster, a dog, a horse, a gerbil, a goldfish, and a cat. She even had a pet rock (*smile*), but without a doubt, the pet that I remember most was her rabbit. I think I was about 14 at the time, and my sister was about 10 when she got the rabbit. She kept it in a cage in the garage, so I'd have to pass by it every day when I got home from school.

It wasn't long before I started to feel really bad for the rabbit, all cooped up in its cage day after day, all by itself. Finally, one day when my parents were out doing something with my sister, I decided to help set this poor rabbit free. I nervously grabbed the rabbit's cage, took it out to the backyard, opened the door and quickly ran back inside. About 45 minutes later, I came back outside, but much to my surprise the rabbit was still in the cage. Now, being really motivated (and even a bit agitated), I grabbed the rabbit out of its cage, placed it at the edge of the woods and ran back inside the house. This time a couple hours had passed when I realized that my parents would be home soon, and they would realize what I had done because I had left the empty cage in the backyard. So once again, I ventured into the backyard and wouldn't you know it, when I went outside there was my sister's rabbit right back in its cage!! The only thing that would have surprised me more is if her rabbit would have figured a way to shut the cage door behind itself.

Do you know that whole thing took place over forty years ago, and to this day, I still don't know why that rabbit went back into its cage? Maybe it was afraid of what was outside of the cage. Maybe it had gotten extremely comfortable with its life in captivity, or maybe just maybe, it didn't recognize the opportunity that it had been given for a better life. I say all this because some of you reading this are like my sister's rabbit. By that I mean you have let fear or being comfortable with where you are at keep you from (or you are just completely unaware of) the opportunity and door that God has opened up for you for a better life.

As I stated in the intro, there are going to be some very real obstacles and oppositions in order to get to where God wants to take you. That is in large part because we have an enemy that wants to do everything in his power to keep you from EVER reaching your full potential. As any person that is currently maximizing their potential will tell you, there is no easy way and no shortcuts to any place worth going. With that said, let's get back to the Bible and take a look at some of the obstacles you are likely going to face along the way.

WILT THOU BE MADE WHOLE?

> *And a certain man was there, which had an*
> *infirmity thirty and eight years. When Jesus saw*
> *him lie, and knew that he had been now a*
> *long time in that case, he saith unto him, Wilt thou*
> *be made whole? The impotent man answered him,*

Sir, I have no man, when the water is troubled,
to put me in to the pool: but while I am coming,
another steppeth down before me.
John 5:5-7

The Scripture doesn't say if the man with the infirmity knew Jesus or not, but even if he didn't, I find it hard to believe that he hadn't at least heard word of the young Rabbi who was going around healing the sick, raising the dead and doing many miraculous works. With that said, the man's response is puzzling. Jesus didn't ask him "why aren't you whole?" but rather "Do you want to be made whole?" I don't know about you, but if I had been in bondage to an ailment and Jesus walked up to me and asked if I wanted to be made whole, I wouldn't hesitate; I'd be like "Yes Jesus, more than ANYTHING!" Especially if I had been in that condition for 38 years! But that wasn't this man's response, was it? Instead of responding with excitement, he replied with excuses. Basically, he told Jesus (and probably anyone else that would listen) what he saw as all the obstacles standing in the way of him being made whole or complete.

Thing is whether it is this man with a condition or my sister's rabbit with its cage and confinement, you can find yourself in a bad situation or state so long that you don't even recognize when a door is being opened for you to get out of that place. This brings me to some of the obstacles each of us will face in trying to walk in our maximum, God-given potential.

OBSTACLE 1– DEFEATED (NEGATIVE) MINDSETS

If you think you can or think you can't,
you are right either way.
Edwin Cole & Henry Ford

I recently saw a documentary on how they train elephants. It was extremely hard to watch. The baby elephants, which weigh around 200-300 pounds, have a metal cuff attached to one of their front legs. That cuff is then attached to about a 40–50 foot metal chain that basically has what amounts to a 20 pound tent peg at the end of it. That tent peg is then pounded into the ground, holding the elephant in place.

Day after day the young elephants would struggle, unsuccessfully, to break free from their bondage. Fast forward a couple of years and the baby elephant is now full grown and weighs a couple of tons. It still has a metal cuff around its leg, obviously a bigger version, but same 40–50 foot chain and yes, the same 20 pound tent peg holding it in place. Now you may be asking, can a 20 pound tent peg really hold a powerful, two to three-ton elephant captive? I think we all know the answer to that is absolutely not. But here's the thing, the elephant doesn't know that. See all the times the baby elephant tried and failed to break free from its captivity had conditioned it to believe that it could never be free of its bondage. Take a moment to examine what it is you have been telling yourself about a situation, sin or sickness in your life that you have been struggling to break free of? Can you see how a negative mindset can not only keep you bound, but keep you from even trying to break free? And we wonder why we are not living up to our full potential.

OBSTACLE 2– RELIGIOUS (PROTOCOLS) MINDSETS

> *For an angel of the Lord went down at certain*
> *seasons into the pool, and stirred up the water;*
> *whoever then first, after the stirring up of the water,*
> *stepped in was healed of whatever disease he had.*
> John 5:4 ESV

> *And the ruler of the synagogue*

answered with indignation, because Jesus
had healed on the Sabbath day, and said unto
the people, "There are six days in which men
ought to work: in them therefore come and be
healed, and not on the Sabbath".
Luke 13:14

It is probably going to come as a surprise to many of you reading this, that a Christian author, writing a faith-based book would ever have the audacity to say that religious protocols and mindsets can be a major obstacle to living your best and blessed life, but it is true. We just read about a man who struggled with an infirmity for 38 years. In fact, we hear in his words that he was so focused on the religious protocol and practices in place (how and when to get in the water to receive his healing) that he almost missed his miracle! Although discouraging, he is not alone in that regard.

There was a man in the Scriptures named Namaan, a commander in the Syrian army, who had leprosy. He almost missed his healing because his religious mindset told him that the man of God would make a big, dramatic show of healing him. So, when he was told he simply needed to just go and wash himself in the Jordan river seven times, he got angry.[1] See there are countless people around the world that have bought into the religious mindset that if you show up on a certain day and pray or do things a certain way, then God must bless, heal, or deliver you. Extremely dangerous and potentially discouraging, as what happens when God doesn't do what your religious protocol or mindset promises you that He has to do?

There is no greater example of religious mindsets getting in the way of the miraculous power of God than the Pharisees. It is bad enough that the passage above shows how they equated the miracle working power of God to the work of men. The Scriptures also record countless examples of these "religious leaders" persecuting, slandering, and even plotting against Jesus.[2] And why? All because He didn't adhere to many of their legalistic, religious protocols and practices. Basically, Jesus ate with tax collectors and sinners[3] and healed people on the Sabbath.[4] The Pharisees even came against the disciples of Jesus for not fasting enough,[5] plucking ears of corn on the Sabbath,[6] and not practicing ceremonial washing.[7]

Now don't get me wrong and go around telling people that Brother Mike said that all religious and church mindsets and practices are bad or wrong. Not what I am saying at all. What I am saying though, is that when we exalt or put our faith in those religious mindsets, methods, practices, and protocols above our personal relationship with God, then that is a problem. So, if you find yourself equating receiving healing, blessings, and the miracle working power of God into just following a certain formula, format, ritual, or routine, watch out that you don't miss out, like the Pharisees.

OBSTACLE 3– UNBELIEVING MINDSETS

Now He did not do many mighty works
there because of their unbelief.
Matthew 13:58 NKJV

In case you are not familiar with this passage, the person that this Scripture is referring to, "not doing many mighty works (aka miracles), is Jesus. That's right, water walking,[8] leper healing,[9] multitude feeding,[10] water into wine changing,[11] blind eye opening,[12] dead raising Jesus.[13] What was the reason given that He did not do many mighty works? Because of their **unbelief**.

There is no better example of how an unbelieving mindset can cause you to miss out on the blessings that God has for you, than the Israelites.

God promised them a great land, flowing with milk and honey[14] (signifying abundance), and God confirmed His promise to the Israelites through many signs and wonders.[15] Including parting the Red Sea for them to cross through and closing it in on top of their enemies,[16] to delivering them from 400 years of bitter bondage.[17] Yet even after all that, they still doubted and didn't trust God to do what He said He'd do and what He promised, He'd bring to pass.[18] How many times have we done the exact same thing?

While faith is not the currency by which we purchase the blessings of God, it is the conduit by which the power of God flows through. The Scriptures bear witness to this as practically every healing or miracle Jesus did was accompanied by faith being put into action. The woman with an issue of blood, who received healing by just touching the hem of Jesus' garment,[19] a paralytic taking up his bed and walking,[20] Peter walking on water[21] and pulling in a net-breaking catch of fish.[22] We know that faith in action, played a huge role in these miracles as Jesus himself is quoted as saying the following: "Your faith has made you well," to the woman with the issue of blood,[23] and "According to your faith let it be to you," to a couple of blind men that received their sight.[24]

After reading this, do you recognize any areas of your life where you have let an unbelieving mindset hinder or hold you back from seeing the miracle working power of God in your life? Maybe you are like a lot of people that have a wrong view of God. They believe in a God who can, but are not sure if He is a God that will or wants to. If this is speaking to you, then I suggest you look to the cross. God did not spare His own Son but delivered Him up for us all. Will He not also with Him graciously give us all things? So, are you going to take God at His Word, believe and receive, or will you continue to settle for less, doubt, and miss out on the abundant life that Jesus has promised you?[25] This brings us to our last obstacle:

OBSTACLE 4– HATER MINDSETS

But it so happened, when Sanballat heard that we
were rebuilding the wall, that he was furious and
very indignant, and mocked the Jews. And he spoke
before his brethren and the army of Samaria and
said. "What are these feeble Jews doing? Will they
fortify themselves? Will they offer sacrifices?
Will they complete it in a day? Will they revive
the stones from the heaps of rubbish-stones that
are burned?" Now Tobiah the Ammonite was beside
him, and he said, "Whatever they build, if even a
fox goes up on it, he will break down their stone
wall." Hear, O our God, for we are despised; turn
their reproach on their own heads, and give them
as plunder to a land of captivity!
Nehemiah 4:1-4 NKJV

Have you ever noticed when you are trying to do something good, positive, or godly you will get all kinds of opposition, resistance, or even just negative, discouraging commentary? Funny thing is, the times when I have gone out and done something stupid, selfish, or even sinful I didn't face any opposition at all. In fact, often I would be cheered on or congratulated for doing stuff that was dumb, dangerous, or detrimental to my future. Why is that? Well, the world will tell you that misery loves company, but I honestly believe whenever someone steps up and pursues a better life for themselves it really makes those that are not doing that uncomfortable. It is like if two friends are both overweight and one of them loses a hundred pounds. The friend that didn't lose the weight is probably going to be inwardly upset with themself that they didn't lose weight as well. They are also likely to be a little jealous, which will likely come out in the form of some resentment or negative commentary. This is because it is always easier to pick at or put down someone else's success, than it is to take a hard look at ourselves and see why we aren't getting the same results.

You need to know that there will be some "haters," "naysayers," and "discouragers" (basically Sanballats and Tobiahs) on the road to your best and blessed life. Which I can tell you from firsthand experience can be extremely detrimental and discouraging to reaching your destination. Sadly, some may even be of your own household,[26] meaning friends, family members, or brothers and sisters in Christ. Don't shoot the messenger, just trying to prepare you for what's coming.

So, we started this section with a biblical account about a man named Nehemiah who was inspired by God to rebuild the walls of Jerusalem that lay in ruins. What did he get in return for stepping up and stepping out in faith and trying to do a good and godly thing? Threatened, criticized, viscously opposed, mocked and ridiculed. This isn't an isolated incident though; the Bible is full of accounts like that. There is an account of a blind man who heard that Jesus was passing by and cried out for Him to have mercy on him.[27] You would think that the crowd that was there would help or at least encourage this man in need to get to Jesus, but you would be wrong. Instead they warned him to keep quiet and not to bother Jesus.[28] Then there was a time when a group of children were brought to Jesus that He might put his hands on them and pray, but His disciples, instead of helping the children, rebuked them.[29] Even Jesus on His way to fulfilling God's purpose for His life was rebuked by Peter for saying that He would have to suffer many things from the religious leaders and even be killed.[30]

In closing I want to leave you with a few words of encouragement for the times you are facing some of these obstacles that we covered in this chapter. First, you need to know that despite the fact that many are the afflictions of the righteous, the Lord promises to deliver you from them all.[31] And even though the Scriptures proclaim that all who will live godly lives in Christ Jesus will suffer persecution[32] and that we will have to go thru many tribulations in this life,[33] the good news is that all of these obstacles are just temporary and Heaven is our reward. So, when discouragement tries to come in, just keep your eyes on the prize and remember this short poem:

When long and steep the road appears
and heavy is the task,
Our Heavenly Father says, "Press on my child
one more step is all I ask."
Unknown

Do you relate more to my sister's rabbit (being stuck in a situation so long that you don't know anything else, or even recognize when a door has been opened to you)? Or do you see yourself more in the story about the elephant (basically tried everything to get free, but you finally just gave up)?

PERSONALLY APPLYING CENTRAL TRUTH

Which mindset do you see being the biggest obstacle to you reaching your goals and God-given potential? Below are some Scriptures to combat each one.

1– Defeated (negative) mindsets. Philippians 4:6-8, Philippians 4:13

2– Religious (protocol) mindsets. James 1:26-27, Romans 8:32

3– Unbelieving mindsets. Mark 9:23-24, Mark 11:22-24

4– Hater mindsets. John 15:18-25, Matthew 5:44, Romans 12:21

CHAPTER 9

DO YOU KNOW GOD?
(AND DOES HE KNOW YOU?!)

No God, no peace.
Know God, know peace.
Billy Graham

I am sure you probably have a favorite athlete, actor, actress, and even author (don't worry; I won't get upset if it's not me- yet.) You may have watched all their games, seen all their movies, and read all their books. You may even know practically everything there is to know about them, but since you haven't spent any real time with them, you don't really know them, right? Same can be true with God. You may have been raised in a God-fearing household, gone to church, wear a cross, and read the Bible, but while you may have learned all about God doing those things, that doesn't mean that you really know Him. There is a big difference between knowing about someone versus truly knowing them.

Hopefully, you haven't had to learn this lesson the hard way, like I did by having a fiancée, family member, and even some friends that I thought I knew, show a different character when something happened (got sick, got locked-up, inherited some money, etc.) and suddenly I found out that I never really knew that person at all.

DO YOU KNOW GOD?

Now the sons of Eli were corrupt;
they did not know the Lord.
1 Samuel 2:12

(Now Samuel did not yet know the Lord, nor
was the word of the Lord yet revealed to him.)
1 Samuel 3:7 NKJV

Eli was a priest in Shiloh, which was located about 20 miles north of Jerusalem. Shiloh was the religious center for the Israelites and location of the *Ark of the Covenant*, at the time this was written. Eli's sons also served as priests.[1] A woman named Hannah cried out to God for a child and promised that if God would give her a son, then she would dedicate him to God for lifelong service.[2] God answered her prayer and Hannah honored her vow and dedicated her son Samuel to the Lord.[3] Scripture says, "Samuel ministered to the Lord before Eli the priest."[4]

What do these individuals (Eli's sons and Hannah's son Samuel) have in common? Even though they all ministered unto God in Shiloh alongside Eli, the Scripture is very clear that THEY DID <u>NOT</u> KNOW GOD! Now you would think that being a priest, growing up in a godly household, having a father that was a priest, ministering unto God in Shiloh, or having a mother who cried out to God would mean that surely you knew God, but again you would be wrong. I can relate as I was pretty much raised up in church as a child (Sunday school, catechism, altar boy, etc.), but in reality the God in my head, who I was serving was more of a game show host, genie in a bottle, or 9-1-1 operator than the Almighty God of the Scriptures. So, you can **learn all about** God and still **not know God.** I say that because I did just that growing up.

Contrast that with Solomon, whose father David told him to "Know thou the God of thy father, and serve him with a perfect heart and with a willing mind,"[5] and Job who said, "I know that my Redeemer lives."[6] Here you have two men seemingly at opposite ends of the spectrum; Job who suffered from losing everything (his house, health, children, etc.)[7] and King Solomon who suffered from having everything (riches, fame, possessions, wives, etc.)[8] but despite their vastly different life stories, they had one thing in common, **they both KNEW GOD!**

Now, when I talk about *knowing* God, the word is from the Hebrew word *yada*,[9] which means having an intimate, personal knowledge of God. It is the same word used when the Bible says that Adam knew his wife Eve.[10] So, do you *yada* (know) God or just know about Him? Before you answer, let's take a look at what the Scriptures lay out as clear evidence of whether or not a person really knows God.

EVIDENCE 1– KEEPING GOD'S COMMANDMENTS

Now by this we know that we know Him,
if we keep His commandments. He who says,
"I know Him," and does not keep His commandments,
is a liar, and the truth is not in him.
1 John 2:3-4 NKJV

Hopefully after Chapter 2 *I'm Not That Bad, Am I?* you can at least name some of the Commandments now? This passage seems to lay out a pretty clear-cut indication of whether you know God or not, keeping His Commandments. So how have you been doing with keeping the Commandments this year, this month, and this week? How about just today? Have you kept all of them or just some? Just so you know the Scripture says that a person who breaks even one of the Commandments is guilty of all.

Even though the Word says God's Commandments are not grievous,[11] there are probably some of you that are saying, "I cannot possibly keep all Ten Commandments every single day," especially since we are talking about keeping the spirit of the Commandments and not just the letter. So, let me simplify it for you, how are you doing with the modified version of the Commandments that Jesus gave us? Basically, to love the Lord thy God with all your heart, soul, mind, and strength, and to love your neighbor as yourself.[12]

See rather than focusing on what we are NOT supposed to do, Jesus is trying to get us to focus on what TO DO. As He knows when we turn our relationship with Him into religious duty and obligation; the mindset "have to" and don't do" (a recipe for falling away) versus the mindset "get to" and "want to" (freedom). Truth be told, when we really strive to love God with all our heart, mind, soul, and strength, then we will not have other gods before Him, we won't use His name in vain, etc. (basically the first five Commandments). Likewise, when we love our neighbors as ourselves, we will not steal, kill, commit adultery, etc. (basically the last five Commandments). All of which leads us to living our best and truly blessed lives!

EVIDENCE 2– OUR LOVE

> *Beloved, let us love one another, for love*
> *is from God; and everyone who loves is born*
> *of God and knows God. The one who does not*
> *love does not know God, for God is love.*
> 1 John 4:7-8 NASB1995

If you were to ask most people how they know if someone is a Christian or not you would probably get the following answers: I know someone is a Christian if they go to church, wear a cross, carry or read a Bible, etc. Some may even believe someone is a Christian if they wear a

Christian t-shirt or have one of those Christian bumper stickers on their car. But the Bible is clear on how all people will know you are a Christian, and not coincidentally, it's the same evidence that a person really knows God; it's by our love.[13] This really should not come as a big surprise, especially in light of the fact that God doesn't just show love, HE IS LOVE![14]

There are all kinds of love mentioned in the Scriptures. In the Hebrew there is *ahab*- deep affection/marital love,[15] *rayah*- companion love,[16] and *dowd*- caress/physical love.[17] In the Greek there is *eros*- intimate love,[18] *phileo*- friendship/brotherly love,[19] and of course *agape*- benevolent/divine/unconditional love.[20]

So how is your love these days? Now when I say that I don't just mean how is your love for your spouse, significant other, siblings, children, friends, or in general for those that love you. Jesus says that even tax collectors and sinners have that kind of love.[21] What I am really asking is how your love is for your neighbors, strangers, other Christians, and your enemies? Yes, God calls us to love them too! In fact, the Scriptures make the importance of loving others crystal clear when it asks the question, how can we love God who we don't see, if we can't even love our brothers and sisters that we do see.[22]

You may not realize this, but the only reason you can even love in the first place is because God first loved you.[23] And just for the record, a good definition of love is giving to others at the expense of self, as opposed to lust which desires to get for self at the expense of others. Which is confirmed by one of the most widely recognized Scriptures of all time, "For God so loved the world that <u>He gave</u> His only begotten Son, that whoever believes in Him should not perish but have everlasting life."[24]

If all of that doesn't convince you as to the importance of love, then 1 Corinthians 13, widely acknowledged as the "Love Chapter" warns us that you can have more degrees than a thermometer, speak more tongues than a United Nations translator, give more money than Bill Gates and Oprah combined, and even give your body to be burned for your faith, but if you don't have love it doesn't mean a thing and you don't really know God.

EVIDENCE 3– BEING KNOWN

> *And the evil spirit answered and said,*
> *"Jesus I know, and Paul I know; but who are you?"*
> Acts 19:15 NKJV

I am sure that I am not the only one who has spent much of his life trying to "fly under the radar", right? Which begs the question, whose radar are we trying to fly under: God or the devil? The passage above is quite interesting. There was a Jewish chief priest named Sceva who had seven sons.[25] One day they took it upon themselves to go out call the name of the Lord Jesus over those who had evil spirits, in an attempt to cast out the evil spirits. Sounds like a good work, amen? So, they said "We exorcise you by the Jesus whom Paul preaches."[26] The response they got from the evil spirit was really telling, as it said that it "knew" Paul and Jesus, but not them.[27] Just so you know the result of posing as followers of Jesus, was that they got overpowered and beat up by the man with the evil spirit. In fact, the Scripture says that they all ended up fleeing from that house naked and wounded.[28] I say this to say, does the devil and his troops know that you know God? When you step out of your house, does an alarm sound in the enemy's camp that a mighty man or woman of God is on the move? If not, then you probably don't know God.

Therefore by their fruits you will know them.
Matthew 7:20 NKJV

Another valuable lesson I learned from all that time spent with my mom in her garden is that when you plant a tomato seed, it will produce tomatoes and not cucumbers. If you plant an apple tree, it will produce apples and not grapefruits. That is because there are some biblical principles at work. First of which is a seed will only produce after its kind and a tree will be known by its fruit.[29] Secondly, a good tree cannot produce bad fruit.[30] See when you say that you are a Christian or that you "know God" people are expecting to see some Christian fruit. It is no different than when my mom would place the carrot seed package on a stick in her garden, right next to the row of carrot seeds she had just planted. Anyone looking at that label would expect to see some carrots growing there at some point. Same is true with us that wear a cross, go to church, or claim to be Christians.

If you are professing to be a Christian or to really know God, but aren't producing godly fruit in your life then you may want to take a few moments and examine what kind of tree you really are? After reading this, a good indicator that you know God is that you shouldn't have to go around telling people (or even the enemy) that you know Him or that you're a Christian. They should already know! If they don't, you may be fooling yourself about really knowing God!

Hopefully, this section has given you some clear evidence on whether or not you know God. Now let's flip things around and ask an even more important question...

DOES GOD KNOW YOU?

> *Not everyone who says to Me, 'Lord, Lord,' shall*
> *enter the kingdom of heaven, but he who does the*
> *will of My Father in heaven. Many will say to Me*
> *in that day, 'Lord, Lord, have we not prophesied*
> *in Your name, cast out demons in Your name, and*
> *done many wonders in Your name?' And then I will*
> *declare to them, 'I never knew you; depart from*
> *Me, you who practice lawlessness!'*
> Matthew 7:21-23 NKJV

You are probably wondering, what Brother Mike is thinking asking me, "Does God know you?" I admit that on the surface it sounds like a really silly question, especially in light of the fact that God is *omnipotent, omnipresent,* and *omniscient,* basically meaning that God is *ALL Powerful,*[31] *ALL Present,*[32] and *ALL Knowing.*[33] But remember the "know" we are talking about is a personal, intimate knowledge that comes from having a real relationship with someone.

Plus, don't forget the words of Jesus we just read that clearly indicate there will be <u>many</u> (not just a few) that will come to him on that last day with what sounds like an impressive church resume (prophesied, cast out demons, did many miracles), only to have the Lord say, "Depart from me, I never knew you!" If that doesn't cause you to sit up and take notice of just how important this subject is, then I don't know what will! Here's the thing, and I'm going to keep harping on it because there are eternal ramifications; doing a whole bunch of **good works** and knowing **about** God doesn't mean a thing when this life is over if God never really knew you, and didn't have a personal relationship with you!

We have spent a fair amount of time looking at the evidence on how we know whether we know God. Before I close, I want to leave you with some biblical evidence on whether God knows you.

Jesus says, "My sheep hear my voice, and I know them, and they follow me."[34] The Scripture also states that, "Nevertheless the solid foundation of God stands, having this seal: "The Lord knows those who are His," and "Let everyone who names the name of Christ depart from iniquity."[35]

Are you sure that you are one of His sheep? Do you recognize His voice when He speaks, whether it is through His Word, a sermon, a dream, or another Christian? Lastly, have you departed from a lifestyle of iniquity? If the answer is "no" or "not sure" there is still good news for you; we have a God who can be known, and desires to personally **know you**!

After reading this are you more or less sure that you know God and that God knows you?

What evidence is there to back up your belief? (Are you loving, keeping His Commandments, known by others for being a child of God, and are you hearing His voice?)

Ask a couple people (such as a friend, family member, and co-worker) to list three characteristics they associate with you? (Make sure to ask them to please be brutally honest in their assessment.)

Are loving, kind, or charitable on any of the lists? If not, read 1 Corinthians 13 and make a commitment to work on embodying the characteristics of godly love listed.

CHAPTER 10

DECISIONS, DECISIONS, DECISIONS

*Multitudes, multitudes in the
valley of decision: for the day of the Lord
is near in the valley of decision.*
Joel 3:14

How many decisions do you think you have made today? 100, 1,000, 10,000? Possibly more? When I say decisions, I am not just talking about the serious, life-altering, potentially life and death decisions we are all faced with from time to time. I am sure you have probably had a few of those; really big decisions like whether or not to get married, have children, to drive home from that party you were drinking at, where to live, should you buy or rent a house, or what kind of treatment to get for your cancer, etc.

How about those seemingly mundane decisions we are all faced with on a day-to-day basis? Stuff like what to eat, what to wear, whether to go to work today, and what to do when work is over? When you stop and think about it, even within those minor decisions are a multitude of other decisions, right? Like what are you going to have for breakfast (or for some, whether there is even time for breakfast)? Do I put jam on my toast, what to take a bite out of first, the eggs, bacon, or pancakes? (For me it is the bacon!) Whether to have coffee, juice, or milk? Even when to wipe your face or what to do with the dishes, wash them or just leave them in the sink for later?

Then on your daily drive I am sure you are faced with countless other decisions such as: what radio station to listen to, whether to turn on the heater, or roll down the window? What route to take, when to brake or speed up to pass someone, even whether or not to honk your horn at someone that just cut you off? Hopefully, you will refrain from honking (or cursing) and just show some grace instead, amen?

The point I am trying to make is, that while many of these decisions can seem rather insignificant in the moment, over time they all end up determining what kind of life you will have. You are probably saying to yourself, "What does he mean?" Well, consider something as small as deciding to eat a pastry for breakfast or smoking a cigarette this morning, not that big of deal, right? But what if you make that same decision for the next 20 or 30 years? Think there won't be some consequences and repercussions with your health from that little decision each morning? Now consider the flip side of that scenario; instead of having that pastry and smoke this morning, you decide to start your day off with a little prayer and reading a Scripture. What do you think the benefit and blessing of that would be if you were to decide to do that instead for the next 20 to 30 years? Do you get my point?

I say all this because at the end of our lives we are all just a sum of the decisions that we make each day. Those decisions, no matter how small are inevitably either taking you closer to or farther away from your best and blessed life.

INDECISION IS A DECISION

> *Even if you're on the right track, you'll*
> *get run over if you just sit there.*
> Will Rogers

Do you sense that you are at a crossroads in your life? Are you facing a major decision regarding your finances, family, marriage, career, or just life in general and don't have a clue as to which way you should go? If you're wondering how I know that, relax I haven't been following you around and I'm not reading your mind or your mail. The truth is, I have just been there and done that myself several times.

I certainly know that it can be challenging, even a bit overwhelming to have to make a major life decision that will affect not only you, but those you love as well. Especially, when the right way to go or result of that choice is unclear. Should I go back to school or quit my current dead-end job (which is barely paying the bills and offers me no chance for advancement)? Should I start a new career or even my own business? Should we try and have another child now or wait until our first child is in school? With interest rates rising, is now a good time to buy a house or should we just remodel our current one? Should we get a divorce, seek some counseling for our relationship, or just hope things get better? How can I improve my relationship with my kids? How do I care for my aging parents? How can I quit smoking, lose some weight, and get in better shape? Where will I ever be able to get the money to send my kids to college? Am I doing what God wants me to do with my life? Maybe you are even thinking how much longer can I put off making this decision until everything falls apart?

Do any of those thoughts sound familiar? I don't know about you, but I think I felt my blood pressure increasing and a few more of my hairs turning gray just writing all that! If you are anything like me the next thing you will do is to start running through all the worst-case scenarios of each of those decisions in your head, right? And all for what? In the end what does all that time spent worrying or being fearful of what may happen accomplish? Nothing right? If anything, it just paralyzes us.

There is a story about a man sitting on a fence overlooking a giant courtyard full of people. The devil is on one side and Jesus is on the other side and both are calling to the people in the courtyard to come to them. Slowly, one by one, each of the individuals begins to make their decision. Some deciding to go over to the side that Jesus is on, but sadly many others deciding to go over to the side the devil is on. Finally, the last person makes their choice, and the courtyard is completely empty. Shortly after, the devil walks up to the man on the fence and says, "I've come for you." The man looks at the devil and says, "What are you talking about? I sat on this fence the whole time and never made a decision." The devil smiles and says, "I know you didn't, but the fence belongs to me!"

The lesson from this story is that indecision inevitably ends up being a decision and when it comes to spiritual decisions, that indecision can have eternal consequences. So rather than putting off deciding or allowing worry and fear to hinder us from making the right decision, let's turn our focus on how to make good and godly decisions in our lives, amen?

CHOOSE LIFE

> *I call heaven and earth as witnesses today against*
> *you, that I have set before you life and death,*
> *blessing and cursing; therefore choose life,*
> *that both you and your descendants may live.*
> Deuteronomy 30:19 NKJV

I know these days many people tend to get nervous or argumentative whenever someone attempts to make a point in clear, concise terms that something is either this way or that way. Probably a big reason why so many people attack and dislike the Bible, as it is full of clearly defined statements letting you know that you are on one of two paths (the right one or wrong one). Plus, a lot of people tend to like the proverbial "gray areas" of life that justify our sinful lifestyle and choices. You know the ones that would have you believe that there really are no bad decisions, consequences, or absolute truths,[1] but that is all a lie from the pit of hell. We just read a passage in which God lays out a black and white scenario with some clear cut, either or choices and the consequences from those decisions. Life or death. Blessings or cursing. Honestly even Heaven or hell. The funny thing is God not only gives us the choice, but even tells us what to choose (life) and why to choose it (so both you and your family may live), but truth be told we are stubborn creatures, often hell bent on doing things our way,[2] with little to no thought to the long-term repercussions of our decisions.

While God gives us all the freedom to choose, none of us are free from the consequences of those choices. Let's pause for a moment to compare and contrast the fruit and results of making a godly decision versus making an ungodly one:

GODLY DECISIONS	UNGODLY DECISIONS
Life– John 14:6	Death– Romans 6:23
Blessings– Ephesians 1:3	Curses– Jeremiah 17:5
Peace– 1 Corinthians 14:33	Strife– James 3:16
Joy– Romans 14:17	Sorrow– Matthew 8:12
Freedom– John 8:36	Bondage– 2 Peter 2:19
Light– John 8:12	Darkness– Colossians 1:13
Truth– John 1:17	Lies– John 8:44
Rest– Matthew 11:28	Unrest– Luke 11:24
Comfort– 2 Corinthians 1:3	Torment– Luke 16:23-24
Pleasures Forever– Psalm 16:11	Passing Pleasures– Hebrews 11:25
Victory– 1 Corinthians 15:57	Defeat– Hebrews 2:14
Reward– 1 Corinthians 3:8	Punishment– Matthew 25:46
Salvation– Isaiah 12:2	Eternal Damnation- Matthew 25:41
Lifted up– John 12:32	Cast down– 2 Peter 2:4

Healing– Luke 9:11	Sickness– 1 Corinthians 11:30
Refreshing– Acts 3:19	Thirst– Psalm 143:6-7
Glory– Revelation 21:23	Shame– Daniel 12:2
Eternal– 1 Timothy 1:17	Temporary– 2 Corinthians 4:18
Heaven– 2 Corinthians 5:2	Hell– Luke 12:5

WHAT'S WORTH MORE?

While we do not look at the things which are
seen, but at the things which are not seen. For
the things which are seen are temporary, but the
things which are not seen are eternal.
2 Corinthians 4:18 NKJV

The Scriptures constantly refer to this life as smoke[3] or a vapor.[4] Basically, we are here today and gone tomorrow. Why is it then that we place so much emphasis on the temporary things of this world and extraordinarily little on the eternal things of God? Only thing I can think of is, we live in such a "live for the moment" world that we have lost perspective on what really matters.

Let's say I was to put a pile of shiny new pennies and another pile of dusty, dull 24 karat gold pieces in front of you. I then proceed to give you a wheelbarrow and a shovel and tell you that you have two minutes to fill up your wheelbarrow from one of the piles. Lastly, I say that you can keep all that you are able to get in the wheelbarrow in those two minutes from the pile that you choose. What would you do? The answer seems obvious. Get to shoveling and fill up your wheelbarrow with the gold pieces, right?! But what if you did not know the value of gold or did not believe that the gold was real? You might very well fill your wheelbarrow with the shiny pennies. That is an accurate illustration of the choice most of us are faced with every day. The shiny houses, cars, jewelry, and things of the world often blind us to the real value of the eternal things that God offers, which to us may seem dull, unattractive, and quite honestly, we aren't even totally sure are real anyway.

Reminds me of one of the *Raiders of the Lost Ark* movies where Indiana Jones (played by Harrison Ford) is trying to find the *Holy Grail* in order to save his father's life. He makes his way into a room filled with cups and only one of them is the Lord's cup (aka the *Holy Grail*) which gives eternal life to those who drink from it. Another man steps up first and drinks from a shiny golden cup covered in precious stones, thinking to himself, "Surely this is the cup the King of Kings would drink from." The man drinks from the cup and dies. The guardian of the *Holy Grail* words it perfectly, "He chose poorly." Then Indiana Jones chooses the humblest, unassuming cup on the table and drinks from it. The guardian then says, "You have chosen wisely." Have you chosen wisely or poorly? If the shiny things of the world are what you are choosing each day you should probably reconsider, otherwise on your last day it will not be the guardian of the *Holy Grail*, but God Himself that tells you, "You have chosen poorly."

WHO DO YOU SAY HE IS?

> *When Jesus came into the region of Caesarea*
> *Philippi, He asked His disciples, saying, "Who do*
> *men say that I, the Son of Man, am?" So they said,*
> *"Some say John the Baptist, some Elijah, and others*
> *Jeremiah or one of the prophets." He said to them,*
> *"But who do you say that I am?"*
> Matthew 16:13-15 NKJV

It should not really come as any surprise that there were so many opinions about who people said Jesus was when He walked the earth. Here it is 2,000 years later and there are just as many, if not more different opinions today about Jesus. Some say He was a prophet, some a teacher, and others say He was just a myth or a real nice guy.

Reason I am writing all this at the end of this chapter is because when this life is over you are going to stand before God and give an account.[5] While you are not going to have to give account for who your parents, partners, or even pastor said Jesus is, you will have to give account for who you said that He is? So since deciding "Who Jesus is" is undoubtedly the most important decision anyone will ever have to make in this life, I want to give you some biblical, historical, and eyewitness testimony for you to consider before you decide.

WHO DOES THE BIBLE SAY JESUS IS?

For those of you that don't know, the Bible is a collection of 66 books that were written by basically 40 different men of God over a couple thousand year period, and despite the fact that none of them knew that what they wrote would one day be put with others writings to form one perfectly harmonious book, the Bible, there are a couple of undeniable common threads throughout the Bible. One is God's redemptive plan for His sinful, fallen creation[6] and the other is that Jesus is God. Consider the following Scriptures:

> *Therefore the Lord Himself shall give you a sign;*
> *Behold a virgin shall conceive, and bear a son,*
> *and shall call His name Immanuel*
> *(which literally means "God with us").*
> Isaiah 7:14

> *For unto us a Child is born, Unto us a Son is given;*
> *And the government will be upon His shoulder.*

And His name will be called Wonderful, Counselor,
Mighty God, Everlasting Father, Prince of Peace.
Isaiah 9:6 NKJV

Then God said, "Let Us make man in Our image,
according to Our likeness;
Genesis 1:26 NKJV

For in Him dwells all the fullness of
the Godhead bodily;
Colossians 2:9 NKJV

But to the Son He says: "Your throne,
O God, is forever and ever;
A scepter of righteousness is the
scepter of Your kingdom."
Hebrews 1:8 NKJV

In the beginning was the Word, and the
Word was with God, and the Word was God.
And the Word became flesh and dwelt
among us, and we beheld His glory,
the glory of the only begotten of the
Father, full of grace and truth.
John 1:1, 14 NKJV

And without controversy great is the mystery of godliness:
God was manifested in the flesh, Justified in the Spirit,
Seen by angels, Preached among the Gentiles,
Believed on in the world, Received up in glory.
1 Timothy 3:16 NKJV

WHO DO EYEWITNESSES SAY THAT JESUS IS?

What year is it? I am guessing you didn't say the year 6,020 or 6,000,020, right? So why is our time counted in B.C. (Before Christ) and A.D. (After Death)? Something significant must have taken place that changed the way we track time. It did, and it was the life, death, and resurrection of Jesus Christ. Let me give you a couple Scriptures from some people in the Bible who knew Jesus personally as to who they say He is:

> *When He saw their faith, He said to him,*
> *"Man, your sins are forgiven you."*
> *And the scribes and the Pharisees began to reason,*
> *saying, "Who is this who speaks blasphemies?*
> *Who can forgive sins*
> *but God alone?"*
> Luke 5:20-21 NKJV

> *And Thomas answered and said to Him,*
> *"My Lord and my God!"*
> John 20:28 NKJV

> *Then, he said to Jesus, "Lord, remember me*
> *when You come into Your kingdom."*
> Luke 23:42 NKJV

> *And they worshiped Him, and returned*
> *to Jerusalem with great joy.*
> Luke 24:52 NKJV

WHO DID JESUS SAY THAT HE IS?

Everything written below are the words of Jesus:

"I am the bread of life."
John 6:35

"I am the light of the world."
John 8:12

"Most assuredly, I say to you,
before Abraham was, I AM."
John 8:58 NKJV

"I am the door."
John 10:9

"I am the good sheppard."
John 10:11

"I am the resurrection, and the life."
John 11:25

"I am the true vine."
John 15:1

"I am the way, the truth, and the life.
No one comes to the Father
except through Me."
John 14:6 NKJV

You probably noticed that Jesus made a lot of "I am" statements. If you don't already know, this is significant because this is who God declared Himself to be in the Old Testament. In Exodus Chapter 3, God is talking to Moses through a burning bush about sending him to deliver God's people, the Israelites, out of bondage. Moses basically says to God, when I say that the God of your fathers has sent me to you and they ask, "What is His name? What shall I say to them?" God answers and says to Moses, "**I AM** WHO I **AM**." "Thus, you shall say to the children of Israel, "**I AM** has sent me to you."[7] So when Jesus said concerning Himself that "I am," He was in fact telling people His true identity as the "I AM" God of the Scriptures!

That is some compelling evidence that Jesus is who He says He is. I could give you countless other prophetic, historical, and even secular eyewitness accounts[8] verifying Jesus' claim to be God. Not to mention, the fact that most of His disciples who walked with Him went to their deaths joyfully proclaiming this truth. I don't know about you, but I can't see them doing that for a lie. There is an amazing book called, *The Case for Christ* by Lee Strobel that does an amazing job of putting Jesus on trial and laying out all the evidence for who He is.

To be honest, if He was not the Lord and Messiah[9] that He claimed to be, then He would have to be a liar, a lunatic, or a legend and not a "good person." Especially considering all the things Jesus said about Himself and letting others worship Him, etc., but you won't find any evidence for Him being a myth, con man, or crazy.

I know I am throwing a lot at you, but I cannot stress enough just how important this decision is. I don't know if you have ever done any algebra before, but what I remember about it is they always wanted you to figure out what "x" was, because once you did that everything else about the problem became easy. But if you got "x" wrong, then it doesn't matter how good you did the rest of the math, your final answer would <u>always</u> be wrong. I say that because same is true with Jesus. Once you get Him right (or get right with Him) everything else falls into place, but if you get Jesus wrong or are wrong about who Jesus really is (aka got the wrong Jesus), then nothing else that you do in this life will turn out right in the end.

Do you have a hard time making decisions?

What do you base your decisions on? Is it on what others tell you is right or what God declares is right?

Have you made a real decision about who Jesus is and are you sure it is the right one?

If you're still not sure about who Jesus is, prayerfully ask God to reveal it to you.

Remember the vision/picture of what your life would look like if you were living up to your God-given potential that I had challenged you to write at the end of Chapter 1 *Where Are You?*

Go back and look at it (and if you never wrote it out, you should probably pause and do that now.) Are the decisions that you are currently making (both big and little) leading you closer to the picture you have written down or further away? If it is further away, I have listed some steps for you to follow next time you are faced with a decision.

<u>Steps to take before making a decision:</u>
Step 1- Come to Jesus. Matthew 11:28, Hebrews 4:16
Step 2- Ask God for wisdom. James 1:5, 1 Kings 3:5-9
Step 3- Seek godly counsel. Proverbs 15:22, 13:10
Step 4- Commit your decision to God. Psalm 37:5, 1 Peter 5:7
Step 5- Trust in the Lord for the outcome. Proverbs 3:5-6, 1 John 5:14-15
Step 6- Wait on the Lord. Psalm 27:14, Isaiah 40:31

CHAPTER 11

FOLLOW ME
(EXCUSES DON'T EXCUSE US)

*After these things He went out and
saw a tax collector named Levi, sitting at the
tax office. And He said to him, "Follow Me."
So he left all, rose up, and followed Him.*
Luke 5:27-28 NKJV

Two simple words "Follow me." No explanations given, no conditions set, no promises made, just Jesus saying, "Follow me." As amazing as the call that He put out to His disciples was, the response was even more incredible. They dropped EVERYTHING they were doing (work, nets, lives) and left EVERYTHING they had (homes, wives, and families) and went without even asking Jesus a single question. Like, where are we going Lord? What will we be doing? Or just how long will we be gone Jesus?

Maybe the answer lies in a closer examination of the question. For starters the word *follow* in the Greek is *Akoloutheo*. *Akolou* means to accompany, be in the same way with, or continue to the end.[1] And *Theo* from the root word *Theos* meaning Jehovah or God.[2] So what Jesus was really asking them was if they would accompany, be in the same way with, and continue to the end with Jehovah God?

Also, we need to remember that most people that came across Jesus addressed Him as *Rabbi*,[3] which basically means teacher or master. I say that because in Jewish culture people recognized that when a rabbi showed up and asked someone to follow them that meant a serious, lifelong commitment.

FOLLOW HIS FOOTSTEPS

> *For to this you were called, because*
> *Christ also suffered for us, leaving us an*
> *example, that you should follow His steps.*
> 1 Peter 2:21 NKJV

There was a man that went to work every day. He would eat dinner with his wife and kids, and then he'd walk down to the bar and get drunk every night. One winter night, the man is at the bar looking out the window at the couple inches of snow that has fallen, when suddenly he sees his five-year-old son standing in the snow outside of the bar. The man runs out and grabs his son and says, "How did you get here son?" The son responds, "I just followed your footsteps dad."

I say that to say, not only are we all following in someone's footsteps, but there is also someone following in ours as well. It may be a brother, sister, son, daughter, niece, nephew, cousin or just some young person that looks up to you. Ruth told her mother-in-law Naomi that she would basically follow her "wherever" she went.[4] King David said to God in the Psalms, "My soul follows close behind You.[5] So, you need to ask yourself several questions: 1– Are the footsteps that you are following taking you closer to or farther away from your best and blessed life? 2– Are the footsteps that you are leaving behind leading others to believe that you are who God says you are?

COUNTING THE COST

> *And whoever does not bear his*
> *cross and come after Me cannot be My disciple.*
> *For which of you, intending to build a tower,*
> *does not sit down first and count the cost,*
> *whether he has enough to finish it.*
> Luke 14:27-28 NKJV

Ever started something new, like a kitchen remodel project, workout routine, business venture, or even weight loss plan and then a little way into it you realize that it was way more work, pain, time, and effort than you had originally thought it would be? Truth be told, while it seemed like a really good idea at the time and something you thought you could achieve relatively easily, you hadn't ever really sat down and counted the cost of what it was going to take to get the job done or reach your goal. Don't feel bad, you're not alone. The same is true of reaching your God-given potential. We have a generation of believer's today that while they love the idea of being blessed, having Jesus in their lives, and a mansion prepared for them in Heaven,[6] they have not ever truly counted the cost of **following** Jesus. There is no better biblical example of this condition, than that of the rich young ruler. Consider the following passage:

> *Now a certain ruler asked Him, saying, "Good*
> *Teacher, what shall I do to inherit eternal life?"*
> *So, Jesus said to him, "Why do you call Me good?*
> *No one is good but One, that is, God. You know the*
> *commandments: 'Do not commit adultery,' 'Do not*
> *murder,' 'Do not steal,' 'Do not bear false witness,'*
> *'Honor your father and your mother.'" And he*
> *said, "All these things I have kept from my youth."*
> *So when Jesus heard these things, He said to*

him, "You still lack one thing. Sell all that you
have and distribute to the poor, and you will have
treasure in heaven; and come, follow Me." But
when he heard this, he became very sorrowful,
for he was very rich.
Luke 18:18-23 NKJV

This passage is probably making quite a few of you reading it a bit uncomfortable, that is the point. On the surface this man seemed to have it all together. You may even think that here is someone that has read this book and who is living up to their God-given potential. He was rich, young, had an important position, and he even professed to have kept all the Commandments from his youth, but when Jesus tells him the cost of being a follower, the passage says that he went away **very sorrowful.** What gives here? It is pretty apparent that even with all the stuff he had going for him, God was no longer on the throne of his heart. Stop and give some serious thought to what you would have said if Jesus were to walk up to you and say, "Come follow me, and oh yeah before you do, go sell <u>ALL</u> that you have (like that big house, those three cars, the boat in the driveway, all that nice jewelry, your family heirlooms, and even that 401k/IRA). And one more thing, I want you to give it all to the poor!" Tell the truth, your first reaction would probably be, "Say what Jesus?"

Before you start thinking God demands that you take a vow of poverty in order to serve Him, you should probably spend some time looking at all the people of God throughout the Bible that God blessed and prospered beyond measure.[7] It is also interesting to note that this is not the approach that Jesus took with the others that He asked to follow Him,[8] but then again it's not hard to see why Jesus said what He said to this particular individual. The rich young ruler obviously loved the stuff in his life, more than he loved the God who gave him the stuff and even gave him his life in the first place! Can any of you relate to that condition? I know there have been times in my life when I have struggled with this very same thing. Yeah, sorry to disappoint you, but I wasn't always saved, and this may shock some of you, but even now as a Spirit-filled, born again follower of Christ who is writing this book, there have still been times in my life I have struggled with making/managing my money and not worshipping it.

See when I did finally surrender my life to the Lord, it immediately cost me half my vocabulary (I am sure some of you reading this know what I am talking about, amen?). It also cost me some movie/entertainment choices, some crude jokes I used to tell, a bit of temporary pleasure from sin for a season, and it even cost me some family members and so-called friends (all of whom suddenly wanted nothing to do with me now that I was a Christian). But here is the thing, with all the love, joy, rest, sense of purpose, forgiveness of my sins, and real peace that I now have in my life for the first time, I can honestly say that if I had to do it over again, I would make that same decision 100 times out of 100!

I say all this to say that despite what many of these modern day "prosperity preachers" are selling people and telling people behind the pulpit, there is still a cost to following Jesus, but you also need to know that there is a greater cost to not following Jesus!

FAN vs. FOLLOWER

Fanatic-adjective and noun (person)[9]

1– One having excessive zeal for and irrational attachment to a cause or position.

2– An ardent devotee.

3– A person who is madly enthusiastic about something, esp. religion.

I am sure we all know someone who is a "fanatic" about something, right? Is it just me, or can they be a little challenging to be around at times? They may be a fanatic about some TV series, a particular political party, an issue they are passionate about (like global warming or the environment), their religion, beliefs, or maybe they are just a fanatic about some particular sports team that they have sworn allegiance to. My youngest son is this way about <u>his</u> football team, the Los Angeles Rams. Yeah, he thinks it is "his team". In fact, if you are reading this on a Sunday or Monday night between August and February then you will probably find him in full-on Rams gear from head to toe and decked out with some crazy blue and gold face paint. I know, what can I say? (I think he gets it from his mother's side of the family. Lol)

While my son and others like him are great examples of fanatics for their passion, Jesus asks for more than that of us. See Jesus wasn't looking for or calling people to be His fans, but to be His followers. The rich young ruler is not the only example of a "fan" of Jesus. The Scriptures are full of them. Like many of those that Jesus fed with the couple of fishes and loaves.[10] Jesus tells them that they were basically just following Him around because they ate of the loaves and were filled.[11] There were also ten lepers who cried out to Jesus to have mercy on them,[12] Jesus told them to, "Go and show themselves to the priests." And it happened that as they went, they were all healed, but only one of them returned to Jesus and gave Him thanks and glorified God for their healing.[13] Even some of the disciples that walked with Jesus, were really fans because when the Lord told them what it would cost to follow Him, the Scripture proclaims, that many of His disciples walked with Him no more.[14]

Are you a *fan-* enthusiastic admirer or a *follower-* committed disciple of Jesus? Still not sure let me give you some fan versus follower characteristics:

FANS OF JESUS	FOLLOWERS OF JESUS
Hearers of the word	Doers of the word
Practices a religion	Pursues a relationship
Church goer	Church grower
Wears their cross everyday	Takes up their cross daily
Of the world	In the world
Owns a Bible	Obeys the Bible
Comes for the meal then leaves	Help with the dishes afterwards
Thermometer (goes w/ temp. in room)	Thermostat (sets the temp. in room)
Seat warmer in church	Soul winner in Christ
Looks the part	Lives set apart
Says "What's in it for me?"	Asks "What can I do for others?"

FIRST LET ME

Now it happened as they journeyed on the road,
that someone said to Him, "Lord, I will follow
You wherever You go." And Jesus said to him,
"Foxes have holes and birds of the air have nests,
but the Son of Man has nowhere to lay His head."
Then He said to another, "Follow Me." But he
said, "Lord, let me first go and bury my father."
Jesus said to him, "Let the dead bury their own
dead, but you go and preach the kingdom of God."
And another also said, "Lord, I will follow You,
but let me first go and bid them farewell who are
at my house." But Jesus said to him, "No one, having

put his hand to the plow, and looking back, is fit for
the kingdom of God."
Luke 9:57-62 NKJV

On the surface this may seem like a harsh response by Jesus. I mean is the Lord really against someone burying their father or saying goodbye to their family? Let's take a closer look. The first person seemed eager to follow Jesus. He even promised to follow Him wherever He went. For the record Peter makes a similar proclamation and even adds that he was ready to go with Jesus "both into prison and to death,"[15] only to end up denying Jesus three times,[16] then going back to his old life after Jesus was crucified.[17] Jesus lets the first individual know that he hadn't realistically counted the cost of a life following Him. Basically, his enthusiasm, based on his feeling at the moment, wouldn't have be strong enough to sustain him during the trials that lay ahead. Jesus warned the would-be follower that He, the Son of Man, did not have even the ordinary comforts of home, like a place to lay His head.

The next two "wannabe" disciples seemingly placed family responsibilities ahead of following Jesus. Their "first let me" or in truth, "me first" statements revealed that they had other priorities that got in the way of truly following Jesus. It also highlights a spiritual condition of many today, that they want Jesus on their timeline and terms. Which is really like telling the Lord, "Yeah I'll follow you Jesus, but after my kids are grown, when I get my house paid off, after I get this big project at work done, or just as soon as I get my life in order."

They want God's blessings but want nothing to do with being obedient to God.[18] Peace, but no persecution,[19] happiness, without any holiness.[20] Christ in their life, but without any real cost, commitment, or change to their day-to-day lives.[21] That's a big problem, as God is looking for individuals that are willing to say yes to going wherever, doing whatever, and leaving whenever He calls them to. Is that you today? If not, what "first let me" thing is keeping you from truly following Jesus?

EXCUSES DON'T EXCUSE US

> *Then He said to him, "A certain man gave a great*
> *supper and invited many, and sent his servant at*
> *supper time to say to those who were invited,*
> *'Come, for all things are now ready.' But they all*
> *with one accord began to make excuses. The first*
> *said to him, 'I have bought a piece of ground, and*
> *I must go and see it. I ask you to have me excused.'*
> *And another said, 'I have bought five yoke of oxen,*
> *and I am going to test them. I ask you to have me*
> *excused.' Still another said, 'I have married a wife,*
> *and therefore I cannot come.'"*
> Luke 14:16-20 NKJV

This section is a bit different from the "first let me" crowd that Jesus said, "Follow me" to, as this passage is worded as an invite to a great supper. In addition, the Scripture above clearly calls the responses of those asked to come as, "excuses." I am sure we have all made our fair share of excuses to avoid doing stuff we really didn't want to do or were just trying to get out of. Compared to some of mine, which quite honestly were mostly lies, like "I'm not feeling good today," "I'm too tired," "I'll try to make it," or the tried and true excuse of kids everywhere, "The dog ate my homework!" The ones listed above actually sound reasonable.

You may not know this, but we have all been invited to the marriage supper of the Lamb.[22] Sadly, just like in the parable above, many will make excuses or even have the wrong garment on,[23] clothed in our own righteousness and not Christ's. The word used here for excuses is *paraiteomai* in the Greek, which means decline, shun, avoid, refuse and reject.[24] In that light, are you declining, shunning, avoiding, refusing, and rejecting God's offer to partake of what He has prepared for you in Heaven?

There was a movie back in the day with Jim Carrey in which he went to a seminar that offered a simple, life altering and transformational formula to success: just say "YES" to everything. The movie was called *Yes Man*. It is a funny movie, but there is a very real spiritual truth behind it. Saying yes to God is the one and only true formula to success! God wants to bless, heal, lead, guide, and direct you, along with restoring, reconciling, and redeeming you. And it all starts with saying yes to Jesus' call to, "Follow Me." Will you be God's "Yes Man" (or Woman) today?

Can you relate to the rich young ruler? By that I mean, is there anything in your life that you love or value more than God? (for example: your wife, children, house, career, possessions, even your own life)

Take some time to think about whom you have been following and who is following you?

Are you a fan or a follower of Jesus? Are there any "first let me" statements or excuses you are using to keep from doing something you know God has said to do, like tithing, going to church, reading your Bible, and telling others about Jesus?

If so, will you say yes to Jesus, commit to quit making excuses and putting yourself first and do what God is telling you to do?

CHAPTER 12

HEART CHECK TIME

For the word of God is living and powerful,
and sharper than any two-edged sword,
piercing even to the division of soul and spirit,
and of joints and marrow, and is a discerner of
the thoughts and intents of the heart.
Hebrews 4:12 NKJV

D o you know the average heart beats approximately 104,000 times a day? That is close to 38 million times a year. Then one day it will beat for the last time. I do not know about you, but I never really give any thought or pay attention to my heart beating unless I've just worked out really hard, I'm really nervous, or I'm feeling some pain or discomfort in the left side of my chest. Which at my age leads me to ask, "Is this normal or should I call someone?" (*Smile*)

When is the last time you have been to a doctor for a routine checkup? If you are anything like me then it has probably been a while, huh? However long it has been since your last visit, you pretty much know that when you get there, they are going to ask you a bunch of questions, probably make you take off some clothing, which is always embarrassing in front of a complete stranger, and then hook you up to some fancy machinery that is going to check out your heart, correct? So, if the heading of this chapter hasn't already given it away (or scared you off), we are going to spend these next couple pages doing a "spiritual" heart check. Just like in the natural, if there is an issue with your physical heart (hardened, clogged, not functioning right, etc.) it is always better to get it diagnosed and dealt with early on, otherwise it could lead to some serious problems down the road. Like a heart attack or heart failure.

EVERY ISSUE IS A HEART ISSUE

Keep your heart with all diligence,
For out of it spring the issues of life.
Proverbs 4:23 NKJV

How many of you know someone that has some serious issues in their life? OK, now that I have broken the ice, how many of you reading this have some issues of your own going on? That is pretty much everyone, right? Maybe your issues are with anger, addiction, debt, depression, relationships, or regret. They could even be issues with your finances, family, or faith. Whatever your issue or issues are, you need to know one thing, every issue at its core is a heart issue.

There is no doubt in my mind that the reason so many of us continue to struggle with the same issues over and over is because we try to deal with the symptoms of our issues and not the source, which is our heart. I mean if you were having pain in the left side of your chest and your left arm was going numb, it wouldn't make any sense to put muscle rub on your chest and start shaking your left arm, would it? No, because those aren't the real issues, they are just symptoms of the heart issue or the heart attack that you were having.

Now when I say the word heart, I am not speaking about the chambered, muscular organ that pumps blood through the entire circulatory system of your body. (Although if it has been a while since you have been to a doctor you should get that heart checked because it's really important too). What I am referring to is from the Greek word for heart which is *kardia*[1] where we get the words cardiac, cardio, cardiology, cardiovascular, etc.

It figuratively means the seat of desires, feelings, affections, passions, and impulses.

The reason I am saying this is because all these issues, whether big or small, are hindering you from reaching your full potential in life. With that said, we are going to give our hearts a thorough check-up today to identify any imminent diseases or defects before it is too late.

WHAT ARE YOU SAYING?

For out of the abundance of
the heart the mouth speaks.
Matthew 12:34 NKJV

There are all kinds of ways to check a heart out in the natural: X-rays, MRIs, EKGs, Stethoscopes (which I don't know about you, but I really hate when that ice cold metal touches my skin). They even have that little clothespin looking thing now that clamps down on your finger when they take your blood pressure. But when it comes to your spiritual heart, there is no more accurate indicator of what is going on in your heart, than what is coming out of your mouth.

This is probably why the Scriptures are full of warnings to be careful about what we are saying. For example: "Whoever guards his mouth and tongue keeps his soul from troubles."[2] "A false witness will not go unpunished, and he who speaks lies shall perish."[3] "Death and life are in the power of the tongue, And those who love it will eat its fruit."[4] "He who guards his mouth preserves his life, But he who opens wide his lips shall have destruction."[5] "In the multitude of words sin is not lacking, But he who restrains his lips is wise."⁶ "He who answers a matter before he hears it, It is folly and shame to him."⁷ "For everyone who curses his father or his mother shall surely be put to death."⁸ "Lying lips are an abomination to the Lord."⁹ "But I say to you that for every idle word men may speak, they will give account of it in the day of judgment."¹⁰ "For by your words you will be justified, and by your words you will be condemned."¹¹

That is just a <u>little</u> glimpse into just how serious God takes what is coming out of our mouths. If you want a more in-depth look at how tough the battle with the tongue really is then I suggest you read the third chapter of the book of James. He basically devotes a whole chapter on the "untamable tongue," in which he describes the tongue as a fire, a world of iniquity, an unruly evil, full of deadly poison and it is set on fire by hell.¹² (And you thought I gave it to you straight). James doesn't play around or sugar coat it at all in his writing!

This is going to date me, but back in the day television would have a seven second delay on live broadcasts. This was to ensure that they had time to edit and bleep out any bad words before they went out over the airways. If you have watched any TV or sporting events recently, then you are going to find out really quickly that they no longer do that. So, before I move on to the next biblical heart check, I want to leave you with some clear indicators of what a healthy heart sounds like versus an unhealthy one. It is no different than the sounds a stethoscope is listening for to see if your heart is in good condition or has some issues that need to be dealt with. Which, when it comes to your spiritual heart means that others shouldn't be hearing irregular sounds like a curse word or murmur if everything is really functioning right inside. Since this is a biblical heart check, I put Scripture next to each sound, so you won't just think it's me that's saying this.

Sounds a Healthy Spiritual Heart Makes:

- Truthful– Ephesians 4:25
- Life– John 6:63
- Thanksgiving– 1 Thessalonians 5:18
- Praising– Acts 16:25
- Gentle– Proverbs 15:1 NASB
- Edifying– Ephesians 4:29

Sounds an Unhealthy Spiritual Heart Makes:

- Lying– Ephesians 4:25
- Death– Proverbs 18:21
- Murmuring– Philippians 2:14
- Complaining– Jude 16
- Harsh– Proverbs 15:1 NASB
- Gossiping– 1 Timothy 5:13

WHAT ARE YOU TREASURING?

For where your treasure is,
there your heart will be also.
Matthew 6:21 NKJV

Another excellent biblical indicator as to the condition of your heart is what you are treasuring. This passage tells me that if we had one of those treasure maps with the big "X" on it from the movies, that it would lead us right to our hearts. Which leads me to ask, if we were to go to that proverbial "X" on the left side of your chest and do some digging what would we find? Would it be God's Word hidden in your heart[13] or would it be something else we would find buried in there? Remember, where our treasure is, our hearts are also.

I know most of us think that we know what is in our hearts, but the truth is we really do not. I won't give you the Commandment test again, but I will ask you this, have you ever acted out of character and lied to, cheated on, or maybe just did something hurtful to someone that you really love? I know, me too! And oh, I was really sorry about it later on. In fact, there have even been a couple of times I have done something and afterwards I couldn't really believe that it was me that had done that in the first place. You too? That is because as the Scriptures proclaim, "The heart is deceitful above all things, And desperately wicked; Who can know it?"[14] Think about that for a moment, God tells us in no uncertain terms that not only will our hearts deceive us, but that our hearts are "<u>desperately</u> <u>wicked</u>!"

Jesus says it best when He says, "Do not lay up for yourselves treasures on earth, where moth and rust destroy and where thieves break in and steal; but lay up for yourselves treasures in heaven, where neither moth nor rust destroys and where thieves do not break in and steal."[15] Later He goes on to sum up why by stating that, "No one can serve two masters; for either he will hate the one and love the other, or else he will be loyal to the one and despise the other. You cannot serve God and mammon (riches)."[16]

Once again, before you go and empty your bank account and put all your possessions on *eBay*, *OfferUp,* or *Craig's List*, God is not against you having stuff. In fact, the Scriptures declare that "A good man leaves an inheritance to his children's children."[17] "For the children ought not to lay up for the parents, but parents for the children."[18] God is against the stuff having you, and those possessions sitting on the throne of your heart. That's why the words "Do not lay up for <u>yourselves</u> treasures on earth" are key to what the Lord is warning us about. Besides, as I can personally attest to, having sadly been to my fair share of funerals, you can't take it with you. Which is probably why I have never seen a U-Haul behind a hearse!

WHAT ARE YOU BRINGING FORTH?

A good man out of the good treasure of his heart
brings forth good things, and an evil man out of
the evil treasure brings forth evil things.
Matthew 12:35 NKJV

So, you know I have to ask, what kind of things are you bringing forth or producing in your life? Good things? Evil things? Not sure? You may even be thinking that you are bringing forth a little of both, right? Problem with that is the Scripture says that every tree is known by its fruit.[19] Also, that a good tree can't bring forth bad fruit and a bad tree can't bring forth good fruit.[20] So, the things you bring forth not only tell others what kind of tree you are, but they also go a long way in revealing the real condition of your heart.

Let me give you a couple of good indicators of what you are bringing forth or producing in your life. Do you remember the assignment I gave you at the end of Chapter 9 *Do You Know God? (And Does He Know You?)*, the one where I had you ask a couple people that know you (such as a friend, family member, and co-worker) to list three characteristics that they associate with you? Let me guess, you decided to skip over that part as well? I forgive you but have to say you aren't ever going to reach your God-given potential if won't even take the time to personally consider, then personally apply the truths and godly principles that are found in each chapter. Since the only place "success" comes before "work" is in the dictionary, I am going to challenge you again to go back and complete the Personally Applying Central Truth from Chapter 9 *Do You Know God? (And Does He Know You?)*.

OK, so hopefully you went back in the book and took care of that. It wasn't as hard as you thought it would be, was it? (It never is). So, were you surprised by the responses you got? I once read that every person has three people they must deal with in their life. 1- the person you think you are, 2- the person others think you to be, and finally 3- the person you really are. The problem usually comes when the person we think we are turns out to be a mile apart from the person that others think we are or even worse from the person that we really are. Think about it for a moment, if you see yourself to be this nice, easy going, giving person or even a Christian, but everyone else sees you as a quick-tempered, hard to be around, stingy person or even worldly individual, then there's a major disconnect there, right?

One of the best gauges on whether what you are bringing forth is good or not, is whether it is fruit that others can enjoy and be fed from? Or is it sour, bitter, rotten, or even plastic fruit? I am sure some of you have seen that plastic fruit before. My mom used to keep a bunch of it in a bowl in the living room. It looks good, but then you try to bite into it and you quickly find it lacks any real substance. The best fruit you could ever produce is certainly the "Fruit of the Spirit," which if you don't remember from Chapter 6 *Fight The Good Fight (Identifying Our Enemy)* and Chapter 9 *Do You Know God? (And Does He Know You?)* is love, joy, peace, longsuffering, kindness, goodness, faithfulness, gentleness, and self-control.[21]

Before I close this out, another couple of things to look at regarding what you are bringing forth are as follows: If everyone was like you, what would the world look like? Would it be better or worse? If you are a Christian the question would be more like if everyone was a Christian like you, would anyone get saved, healed, blessed, or come to know Christ? Lastly, and I am going to warn you in advance that this one really convicted me, if God were to answer every prayer that you have prayed in the last 30 days would anything change in the world or just your world? Ouch, huh? Just some food for thought.

Even if after reading all this and undergoing a spiritual checkup, you are realizing that your heart isn't in the best of shape or needs some work done on it, there's great news. You can start by crying out like King David did in the Psalms, "Create in me a clean heart, O God, and renew a steadfast spirit within me."[22] The word create is from the Hebrew word *bara*.[23] This is the same word God used in Genesis 1:1 when He created the heavens and earth. In fact, throughout Scripture, **only GOD** is the subject of this particular verb.

You can then begin the process of sanctifying or setting apart the Lord in your heart,[24] serving the Lord with a singleness of heart,[25] singing and making melody in your heart to the Lord,[26] and lastly keeping guard or watching over your heart with all diligence.[27] Basically, this is equivalent in the natural of paying attention to the things you take into your body, as they have a direct impact on the health of your heart. In the spiritual, be mindful of what you allow to enter your heart through your ear and eye gates, And the thoughts you entertain because as a person thinks in their heart, so are they.[28]

Hopefully, this section spoke to you like it did to me as I was writing it. We spend a lot of time looking at, worrying about, and maintaining our outward appearance, but God is looking at the heart.[29] The question now is, what are you going to do differently? The Scriptures are clear that you cannot truly have the relationship God desires to have with you or even see the promises that God has given to you come to pass with a hard heart,[30] heavy heart,[31] or half a heart.[32]

What does what you are saying, treasuring, and bringing forth say about the condition of your heart?

Can you see now that all the issues in your life are really heart issues?

Will you try putting your own seven second delay in place for one day to watch what comes out of your mouth? I know it is going to be really awkward at first, but it allows you to give some thought before you speak as to whether what you are about to say is building up or tearing down? Blessing or cursing? Speaking life or death?

Commit to praying for God to create in you a clean heart every morning, guarding what you take into your heart, and putting on the breastplate of righteousness for the next thirty days and see if you don't notice a change in the condition of your heart.

CHAPTER 13

PUT OFF, PUT ON, AND PUT AWAY

If you want something different,
you have to be willing to do something different.
Ed Cole

I f you remember, we started this journey together with a couple of tough questions: 1– Are you currently living up to your God-given potential? 2– Have you accomplished everything that God uniquely gifted and created you for? Pretty safe to say that the answer to one or even both of those questions was no, right?

I also told you in the intro that this book was going to confront all childish mindsets and mannerisms that many of us still have, as well as challenge any areas of our lives that are holding us back from living the abundant life that God has promised us.

I say all that again as these next couple of chapters are going to be where the proverbial rubber hits the road, so to speak. It is like that part of a race that long distance runners call "hitting the wall". Basically, it is the point where you are over halfway there, but starting to wonder, even question, if you have what it takes to keep going and reach the finish line. So, I just want to take a moment before moving on, to encourage you to push through and press on, as you are almost there! Yeah, there are still some hurdles to get over and some work to be done, but you can do it!

Don't just take my word for it, God says you can do ALL things thru Christ who strengthens you.[1] He also declares that "Those who wait on the Lord shall renew their strength; They shall mount up with wings like eagles, They shall run and not be weary, They shall walk and not faint."[2] Lastly, God encourages you to not grow weary in well doing and promises that you will reap a harvest in due season if you don't give up.[3] Since we all know that God can't lie,[4] those are promises you can take to the bank. With that said, let's get our second wind and **finish strong!**

PUT OFF

> *That you put off, concerning your former*
> *conduct, the old man which grows corrupt*
> *according to the deceitful lusts.*
> Ephesians 4:22 NKJV

There was a man in the park with a large block of marble, a hammer and a chisel. A big crowd began to gather around as little by little the master sculptor started chiseling away chunks of marble from the block. Suddenly, a little girl no more than six walked up to the man and said, "Hey mister what are you doing?" The man stopped and said, "I'm making an elephant." The little girl's face got serious for a moment as she thought about his answer, she then asked the man, "But how do you know which parts to remove?" The artist looked at her with a smile on his face and said, "It's simple; I just remove everything that doesn't look like an elephant."

Cute story, but there is a deep, spiritual truth to be learned from it. God's ultimate plan for each of us is to be conformed to the image of His Son.[5] So just like the sculptor in the story, God's desire for each of us is to "chisel away" or remove **everything** that doesn't look like Jesus! After redeeming and saving us, God begins a process called *sanctification.* Basically, that is a big Bible word which means to set apart for God's special use.[6] Thus, the reason the Scriptures tell us to, "Come out from among them And be separate, says the Lord."[7] This is not a call to encourage Christians to isolate themselves from unbelievers; rather it is a warning to discourage compromise with their sinful values and practices.

God knows that imperfect, fallen creatures like us are incapable on our own to live the holy, sanctified lives He has called us to live. This is why believers are given the Holy Spirit, who indwells in us at the moment of salvation.[8] Then by the power of the Spirit, we find the ability to, "abstain from fleshly lusts which war against the soul."[9] Over time as we yield ourselves to God, and as we soberly and vigilantly resist the devil and all his temptations,[10] we will find that God is able to "perfect, establish, strengthen, and settle" us.[11]

Our part in this process begins with "putting off" the old man and his old corrupt ways and deceitful lusts, as well as "laying aside" every weight and the sin which so easily ensnares us.[12] A good visual of this would be to picture a person taking off their old, dirty nasty sin-stained clothes before being washed clean by Christ.

Hopefully, I didn't lose any of you with the use of a couple of big church words like sanctification, salvation, and redeeming. If you haven't noticed, I tend to like to put things in plain, simple terms that are easy to understand. This is why I like to incorporate some personal testimonies and even stories to help paint visual pictures of a spiritual truth or principle. That and it's something Jesus did quite often throughout the Gospels.[13] Now that we have spent some time discussing what we need to "put off" let's move on to our next section.

PUT ON

And that you put on the new man
which was created according to God,
in true righteousness and holiness.
Ephesians 4:24 NKJV

Have you ever taken a bath or a shower and then put on the same dirty clothes you just took off? That's pretty bad, right? I had to do it once when I was helping my dad at his construction company. The family whose house we were remodeling was on vacation in Hawaii and I had spent most of the day either reinsulating the attic or crawling around under the house with all kinds of dirt, bugs, and filth. Needless to say, I didn't want to get back in my truck like that, so seeing how it was a cold wintry day, I decided to take a quick, hot shower in the upstairs bathroom. Problem was I hadn't planned on all that happening and hadn't brought any clean clothes with me. So left with the limited options of driving home naked or "borrowing" some clothes from the homeowner, I ended up putting back on my dirty work clothes and drove home, quickly.

While I am sure most of you are grossed out by that or getting a good laugh from it (or both) I share this story as it really is no different than when we put off our old man and his filthy, nasty, sinful ways, let Christ clean us up, and then go right back to our former "filthy rags"[14] or lifestyles!

I want you to stop and think for a moment all the things you "put on" today: underwear, socks, pants, shirt, dress, shoes, hat, coat, watch, ring, jewelry, etc. If you are like my wife then you are probably spending thirty to forty-five minutes putting on some make-up that you don't really need because you're a natural beauty (sorry honey, but it's true). If it is the holidays, then some of you are probably in the process of "putting on" an extra 10-15 pounds. (*Smile*)

Hopefully after reading about our enemy in Chapter 6 *Fight The Good Fight (Identifying Our Enemy)* all of you are taking some time each morning to put on the "whole armor of God" before leaving the house? I also have no doubt that many of you are putting on a good front or facade that everything is good in your life before you go out in public. Even though deep inside you are secretly wondering how you are going to pay the bills this month or even make it through the day. I only say that because that was me for much of my life, but now I put that phony persona on the "put off" pile each morning. It took a while, but I learned that it is too much work to pretend I was doing great every day. Besides, I only ended up fooling myself, as well as hindering my healing. These days I just "put on" the Lord Jesus Christ,[15] the new man I am in Him,[16] the whole armor of God[17] with the armor of light,[18] and the garment of praise.[19] Then and only then am I ready to head on out the door and face the world! What are you putting on each day?

PUT AWAY

> *When I was a child, I spoke as a child, I understood*
> *as a child, I thought as a child; but when I became*
> *a man, I put away childish things.*
> 1 Corinthians 13:11 NKJV

We already covered a lot of the "childish things" many of us still struggle with on a daily basis in Chapter 4, *Grow Up Already, Would You?* So, I won't spend a lot of time on this section. However, it is a key principle of this book and therefore worth reemphasizing, especially considering the fact, childish mindsets and mannerisms are at the core of many of the issues that we as a community, church, country, and even civilization struggle with.

If you are still not sure what I am talking about, just turn on the nightly news or better yet anything to do with politics. I challenge you to close your eyes for a few minutes and just listen. Tell me it doesn't sound like a bunch of children squabbling on the playground or in the back of a school about how "my dad is bigger than your dad" or "if you don't like it I'll take my ball and go home!" It is ridiculous seeing grown men and women acting like that. The gossiping and teenage mentality bullying that happens at so many workplaces these days or all the cursing, horn honking, and childish antics that take place on the daily commute to and from work, only add to the ridiculousness. Can I get an amen?

The problem is, we are stubborn, set in our ways creatures at our core, that have convinced ourselves that the way we see things or even do things is the **only way** to see or do things. Let me ask you something. Whatever age you are, think back 10 years and tell me if you see things differently now then you did back then? If you are old enough to remember, look back another 10 years and let me know if you saw things differently back then? I would imagine the answer is "yes I definitely see things way differently now than I did back then." (By the way if you don't see at least some things differently now than you did 10 or 20 years ago then I hate to tell you this, but you just wasted 1 or 2 decades of your life!) I say that because when I was a teenager, I didn't know anything, except for cars and girls. In my 20s, I thought I had things figured out. By 30, you couldn't tell me anything, I knew it all. At 40, I started asking some really tough questions, and now in my 50s, I'm beginning to realize just how much I don't know!

Before I close this out, I want to leave you with a little bit of "old man" wisdom from someone that carried around a ton of guilt, regret, and even shame from the past, for way too many years. If you ever genuinely want to get to the ultimate destination that God wants you to arrive at and this book is trying to prod, push, and propel you to one of the biggest things you are going to have to "put away" is the belief that your past will ever turn out differently. That, and put away all the regret, hurt, disappointment, and brokenness some of you are still carrying from things not turning out the way you expected them to. If you didn't know this already, God is under no obligation to do what you want, but only what is right! So, I'm going to close this out with a little poem I wrote in regards to what to do with all those would haves, should haves, could haves that we carry around and are weighing us down and keeping us from our best and blessed lives.

Broken Hopes and Dreams

I gave my box of broken hopes
and dreams to God to mend,
I did this because I'd always heard it said
God was my friend.

Some time passed by and I began
to wonder what went wrong,
If God had truly loved me,
then it shouldn't take this long.

I prayed and read the Scriptures,
paying attention to each verse,
But despite all my best efforts, things hadn't gotten better,
in fact they'd only gotten worse.

At last fed up I snatched back the box
and screamed "How could you be so slow?!"
Just then a voice from Heaven spoke,
"I would have fixed them all my child, but you never did let go!"

DEVELOPING A PERSONAL MISSION STATEMENT

A person with a clear purpose will
make progress on even the roughest road,
while a person with no purpose will make no
progress even on the smoothest road.
Thomas Carlyle

You may not realize this, but as Christians God has given us a mission to complete. Just like in those *Mission Impossible* movies, we have a say in whether we choose to accept that mission. Similar to the assignments that Tom Cruise's character Ethan Hunt would be given, our mission is also seemingly impossible. To know God[20] and to make Him known[21] to a lost and dying world that for the most part wants absolutely nothing to do with God or His Word!

As it turns out being a Christian is not just what we do in church, but even more so, **everything we do outside of it**! That is because the call of God on your life instantly turns everything (your job, your marriage, raising your kids, coaching your kid's softball or soccer team, helping at a homeless shelter, etc.) into a ministry. And for the record the word for *ministry* in the Bible is the same word for *service*.[22] That is because we are not only God's ambassadors,[23] but His agents for change.[24] So, something that I've done to remind me of this solemn responsibility was write my own personal "mission statement" and post it on my mirror.

1– Seek God first before doing anything! Matthew 6:33

2– Strive to see every person how God sees them. Genesis 1:26

3– Maintain godly integrity and character at all times.
2 Corinthians 3:2

4– Treat others how I want to be treated. Matthew 7:12

5– Love my wife as Christ loved the church and gave Himself for it. Ephesians 5:25

6– Love, lead, talk to, and teach my children about God. Deuteronomy 6:6-7

7– Preach the Gospel at all times, to all people (and when necessary, use words). Mark 16:15

8– Do not think too highly of myself. Romans 12:3

9– Listen twice as much as I speak. James 1:19

10– Forgive quickly. Colossians 3:13

11– Keep a sense of humor about everything. Proverbs 17:22

12– Defend those who cannot defend themselves. James 1:27

13– Always give to those in need. Matthew 25:35-40

14– Keep the faith and finish my race. 2 Timothy 4:7-8

Picture yourself being that block of marble and God as the one working on you in the park, has enough been "chiseled away" yet for others to see what you are being made into?

What kind of things do you still need to put off or put away? (Possibly impatience, anger, loneliness lying, worry, bitterness, disappointment, guilt, shame, and regret?)

Will you commit to putting off the old you, putting away any childish ways of talking, thinking, or acting and then putting on the new you every morning?

The mission statement I posted on my mirror started with just one thing, "Seek God first before doing anything!" Then over time I started adding to it. Will you start your own personal mission statement and post it on your mirror as a reminder of who God has called you to be and how He has called you to live?

CHAPTER 14

BORN AGAIN

Jesus answered and said to him,
"Most assuredly, I say to you, unless one is
born again, he cannot see the kingdom of God."
Nicodemus said to Him, "How can a man be born
when he is old? Can he enter a second time into
his mother's womb and be born?
John 3:3-4 NKJV

Would you say that you are a Christian? The reason I ask is a recent poll of individuals professing to be Christians revealed the following:

- 20%– Never attend church. Hebrews 10:25
- 25%– Never pray. 1 Thessalonians 5:17
- 30%– Never read the Bible. Joshua 1:8
- 40%– Don't believe in a real devil. Revelation 12:9
- 50%– Don't believe in a literal hell. Luke 12:5
- 70%– Don't believe the Scriptures are inerrant. 2 Timothy 3:16
- 85%– Never serve in any kind of ministry. 2 Corinthians 5:18
- 90%– Don't know how many books are in the Bible. 2 Timothy 2:15
- 95%– Never lead even one person to Christ. Mark 16:15-16
- 100%– Expect to go to Heaven! Matthew 7:21

Is it just me or does something not line up with those statistics? Christians that don't believe in a real devil or hell, never pray, go to church, read the Bible or share their faith? I just don't find examples of that in the Word of God. I think the problem lies in how we define being a Christian nowadays. You may not know this, but followers of Jesus were first called Christians at Antioch,[1] and believe me, at the time it wasn't a term of endearment. In fact, it was more of an offensive or derogatory label, but before they were called Christians, followers of Jesus were called, "of the Way."[2] Which makes sense as Jesus is "the Way, the Truth, and the Life."[3] If the statistics above or the things that I see that are proclaimed, practiced, and passed off as Christianity these days are any indication, then we have definitely lost our way!

Let me explain. Some may think that because they believe there is a God, have been to church, or were raised in a Christian household that means they are a Christian. Sounds reasonable, but the problem with that logic is that just believing there is a God doesn't save anyone! In fact, the Scriptures say that "You believe that there is one God. You do well. Even the demons believe—and tremble!"[4] and we know they aren't saved! As for the whole going to church thing making you a Christian, need I remind you that the Pharisees practically lived in church, and they were the ones plotting to kill Jesus.[5] Plus, Jesus called them a "brood of vipers"[6] and "whitewashed tombs."[7] If you think that being raised in a Christian household makes you a Christian, you may want to rethink that. Tarzan was raised by apes. He even learned to act like/fit in with them, but that never made him one, right? Same is true of being raised by Christians or in a Christian household. It is great, but even if your dad was a pastor and your mom was the worship team leader, it wouldn't make you a Christian.

Others think that they are Christians because they go to church, read the Word and can quote some Scriptures, but while going to church is also a good thing, it makes you a Christian about as much as going to a garage makes you a mechanic or going to a hospital makes you a doctor. Reading the Word is good but is meaningless if you don't live what you read. Lastly, while quoting the Scriptures can be a powerful weapon in the hands of a child of God, as we discussed in Chapter 6 *Fight The Good Fight (Identifying Our Enemy)*, I would be remiss if I didn't remind you that the devil is chronicled in the Bible quoting Scripture, although not surprisingly he actually misquoted and omitted part of it.[8]

Some people think that they are a Christian because they wear a cross, were baptized as a child, or have done a bunch of good deeds. I don't know about you, but I've seen a lot of people wearing crosses: rap stars, gangsters, heavy metal musicians, celebrities, etc. Does that make each of them a Christian, especially when they are living like the devil every day? I don't think so. This is sad because for many the cross they wear is nothing more to them then a blinged-out piece of jewelry or fashion accessory. Besides, Jesus told His disciples to **take up** their cross daily,[9] not wear one. As for baptism, while it is a powerful, biblical ceremony for believers in Christ, just being sprinkled or even fully submerged in water does not make anyone a Christian. Reason being, if that or any other works that we do saved us, then Jesus would not have had to die on the cross for our sins.[10]

ARE YOU SAVED?

> WARNING: Everything not saved will be lost.
> Nintendo WII quit screen & Almighty God

You may be asking saved from what? Good question. I hate to be the one to break it to you, but you are going to die. It may not be today or tomorrow, it may not even happen for 50 years or so, but just like the person sitting on death row, there is a date set for your departure from this world. Unlike the death row inmate, you just don't know exactly when that date is. But before you let that get you down or depressed, there is still hope. That is because death is not the end of life, it is actually the beginning of eternity. And you need to know that you have an absolute say, while you are still alive, as to where you will spend that eternity.

The Scriptures say that "it is appointed for men to die once, but after this the judgment."[11] Each of us has an "appointment" so to speak with the God of the universe and unlike many of the other appointments we have in this life that we just neglect or skip out on, this is one that you will 100% keep. The Scriptures are also clear that on that day you are going to hear one of two things from God; either "Come, you blessed of My Father, inherit the kingdom prepared for you from the foundation of the world"[12] or "Depart from Me, you cursed, into the everlasting fire prepared for the devil and his angels."[13]

Now while God is a loving and merciful God, He is also a just and Holy God which means that He cannot simply overlook the penalty and punishment our sins require without compromising His Holy character. Since **ALL** of us have sinned and fallen short of the glory of God[14] and the wages of that sin is death[15] as well as separation from God, we are all in desperate need of a Savior and Redeemer! That is where Jesus dying on the cross comes into play. God so loved each of us.[16] that He made Jesus, who knew no sin, to be sin for us so that we might become the righteousness of God in Him.[17] Or to put it in simpler terms we owed a debt we couldn't pay so Jesus stepped in and took our place and paid our debt in full with His blood. The sad thing is how many people go through their daily lives ignorant to the sacrifice that was made on their behalf. The following story really illustrates this point.

There was a man named John Griffith who grew up in the depression era (this is the same time frame I mentioned in Chapter 1 *Where Are You?* that my parents both grew up in). Times were tough and work was hard to come by back then, so he moved his family to Missouri, near the edge of the Mississippi river. He had found a job tending one of the great mechanical railroad bridges they had back at that time, spanning the massive river. His job was to raise the bridge for the splendid ships and bulky barges that would sail through and then mechanically lower the structure for the great trains that roared by.

At noon, with his eight-year-old son by his side, John Griffith raised the bridge as he did every day at that time for the ships that were scheduled to pass through. He and his son then sat on the narrow catwalk to eat their lunch. They were having a great time, when suddenly, John, realized it was 1:05 pm and the Memphis express would be by in just five minutes. So, he ran as fast as he could to the control booth to lower the massive bridge. He looked down to make sure that no ships were in sight, and nothing was below when he saw a horrific sight. His son had fallen off the catwalk and was stuck between the teeth of the giant gearbox that moved the bridge up and down. John Griffith had a heart-wrenching decision to make, with the whistle of the speeding train approaching, he knew there was not enough time to run down and try and pull his only son free from the gears. On the other hand, if he didn't lower the bridge it would cause the train to wreck, sending the four hundred passengers to a watery grave!

John Griffith said a brief prayer asking God for strength then pulled the lever lowering the massive bridge, thereby saving the passengers on the train. Years later when he talked about the decision that he had made, he said the thing that had stuck with him the most was the faces of the people on the train. As all were oblivious to the price his son had paid to spare their lives. He said it made him want to cry out, "Don't you know and don't you care that I just sacrificed my only son for you!"

I share that story because how many of us have been just as oblivious to God's sacrifice of His Son on that cross? How He lived the life we couldn't live and died the death we deserved to die, so that we could be made right with God. This is a perfect segue to the next couple of sections covering why Jesus had to die on the cross and what we need to learn from those on the cross alongside of Him.

WHICH CRIMINAL ARE YOU?

> *There were also two others, criminals,*
> *led with Him to be put to death.*
> *Then one of the criminals who were*
> *hanged blasphemed Him, saying, "If You are*
> *the Christ, save Yourself and us." But the other,*
> *answering, rebuked him, saying, "Do you not*
> *even fear God, seeing you are under the same*
> *condemnation? And we indeed justly, for we*
> *receive the due reward of our deeds; but this Man*
> *has done nothing wrong." Then he said to Jesus,*
> *"Lord, remember me when You come into Your*
> *kingdom." And Jesus said to him, "Assuredly,*
> *I say to you, today you will be with Me in Paradise."*
> Luke 23:32, 39-43 NKJV

I am going to spend some time talking about Jesus on the cross, but before I do, I'm going to need you to do something for me first. I need you to take off your religious glasses for a second. I am sure we all have a picture of Jesus in our minds that we either grew up with or came up with. For many with church upbringings that would be based largely on those watered down, watercolor pictures and portraits in churches across the world of a handsome, blue-eyed Jesus, wearing a loincloth, and basking in a divine light up on the cross.

The problem with that image is that is it not Scripturally accurate. Let me explain. First of all, Roman crucifixion was one of the most brutal, painful forms of execution the world has ever known. In fact, the Scriptures say in regard to Jesus on the cross that, "His visage was marred more than any man, And His form more than the sons of men."[18] That basically means that He was so disfigured that He no longer looked human or recognizable. That's because before Jesus was even on the cross He was bound,[19] beaten,[20] mocked,[21] and spit upon.[22]

Since the Jewish religious leaders didn't have the authority to execute Jesus, they took Him to Pontius Pilate, who was the Governor of Judea, at the time. Pilate, after originally attempting to have Jesus released, instead had Him scourged[23] in an attempt to appease the angry crowd. Scourging was a punishment more severe than flogging or beating and was often life-threatening. It was where a prisoner was beaten with a whip fashioned of numerous strips of leather attached to a handle. The leather strips had sharp pieces of bone and metal tied to them, which could rip and tear one's skin to shreds.

After the scourging, Jesus had a crown of thorns pressed onto His head,[24] and was beaten, mocked and spit on repeatedly.[25] He was then led outside the city to a hill called *Golgotha*, which is an Aramaic word meaning "Place of a Skull"[26] where He was crucified.[27] This means that He was stretched out and His hands and feet were nailed to a cross! A crucifixion so horrible that the Bible says that the earth shook and the sun hid its face.[28] He did all that willingly for our sins,[29] so that we could have right standing with God. Hopefully, now you can see why I asked you to remove your "religious glasses", as this is a far cry from the images we see today of Christ's sacrifice.

Anyways, getting back to the passage of Scripture we just read, often we not only forget just how brutal His death was, but that there were two other criminals crucified next to Jesus. The reason I mention this is these two criminals are a good representation of the two camps everyone on the planet falls into; either the "receive Jesus" camp or "reject Jesus" camp. If this sounds familiar it should, as we covered some of this in Chapter 10, *Decisions, Decisions, Decisions* (remember the individuals in the "fence and courtyard" story?)

The Scriptures accurately record two other men dying on the cross along with Jesus. Both called out to Jesus to save them, but Jesus only told one of them that their eternal salvation was secure. What gives here? Let's take a closer look and see what we can learn from this passage. The first criminal calls out to Jesus to save him. And some of you that have read or heard the Bible ministered are probably saying I thought the Scriptures say that all who call on the name of the Lord will be saved?[30] Well, while it docs say that, the Word of God also says, "How then shall they call on Him in whom they have not believed?" And how shall they believe in Him of whom they have not heard?"[31] See people use or even call the name of Jesus all the time. Sadly, too often, the name of Jesus is used as a curse word, exclamation of pain, surprise, or anger, or they are not even calling on the real Jesus of the Scriptures.

So, looking back on the first criminal's words it is not hard to see that he had no real faith in who Jesus really was, and His ability to save him. This is evident by the words "If you are the Christ" (*or Messiah/ Savior*). We can also see a common error that many who come to or even call out to Jesus make. He wanted Jesus on his terms, which we see in the man's "conditional call" for Jesus to save him by asking Jesus to pull Himself and the man off the cross.

Now let us compare the second criminal's approach to Jesus. We notice that this man took responsibility for his sinful actions that led to his being crucified, even rebuking his fellow condemned criminal. Then, he acknowledged Jesus' sinless perfection when he said that Jesus had done "nothing wrong." Lastly, he called Jesus "Lord" and asked Him to "remember him" when He came into His kingdom. This is critical as the Scripture says, "that if you confess with your mouth the Lord Jesus and believe in your heart that God has raised Him from the dead, you will be saved."[32] All of which leads me to the final part of this section, which are the keys to salvation.

ESSENTIALS FOR SALVATION

> *And he brought them out and said, "Sirs,*
> *what must I do to be saved?" So they said,*
> *"Believe on the Lord Jesus Christ, and you*
> *will be saved, you and your household."*
> Acts 16:30-31 NKJV

What must I do to be saved? The jailer asked the right question. Hopefully after reading this, if you are asking the same question, now you know that the answer is not just to call yourself a Christian, pray, wear a cross, read the Bible, quote some Scriptures, go to church, or do a bunch of "good deeds". While those are all positive, godly things, you should do those things because you are saved, not to save you. Instead, Jesus gives us the answer when He says that YOU MUST BE **BORN AGAIN** TO SEE THE KINGDOM OF GOD.[33]

I'm sure that some of you reading this are like Nicodemus who asked, "How can a man be born when he is old? Can he enter a second time into his mother's womb and be born?"[34] It is not that kind of birth though. I know, I was a bit confused by the term *born again* when I first heard it. But it is a spiritual rebirth similar to the transformation or metamorphosis that a caterpillar goes through to become a butterfly. Without that transformation, the caterpillar can try to look and act like a butterfly, but it is still a caterpillar. The reverse is true as well for those of you that have been born again. When the caterpillar truly becomes a butterfly, it may still occasionally revert to acting like a caterpillar, but that does not change the fact that it's a new creation.[35]

Picture yourself on an airplane filled with people you know. Midway through your flight the pilot of the plane comes over the intercom and announces that the plane is about to crash and no one will survive. Just as you are about to lose all hope the pilot of the plane comes back on the intercom and says that the maker of the plane cares so much about you that he has provided each of you with a parachute under your seat that is guaranteed to save your life. That is some good news and is exactly what the Maker of the universe is letting you know He has provided for each of you!

Let me ask you something, does just knowing that there is a parachute under your seat save you or anyone else? No, it does not. It is only when you put on the parachute, and trust in it completely, that it can save you. Same is true of Jesus. Beware though, (and this is one of the hardest things for me as a Christian who has family members that aren't currently saved) I can't give my kids or my loved ones my parachute or make them put on the one that has been provided specifically for them.

I say all this because as we have already established, you and everyone you know are figuratively on a plane that is going to crash. So my question for you is, do you have your parachute (Jesus) on? If so, are you telling others that may have been asleep or distracted by the in-flight meal or movie, that Almighty God has provided them with a lifesaving gift? If not, **what are you waiting for?**

The world will try and tell you that all roads lead to Heaven, but the question you must ask yourself is will God be happy to see you when you get there? The Scriptures declare that there is only one name under Heaven whereby we must be saved,[36] and Jesus says that no one comes to the Father, except by Him.[37] For those that haven't truly opened the door of your heart to Jesus yet or for those of you that aren't sure that if they died tonight where they would spend eternity, I want to take a moment to simply walk you through the essentials for being born again or saved. This is a life transforming decision with eternal ramifications. Take your time and prayerfully consider the following, as eternity is too long to get wrong!

1– **Recognize** Just as a person needs to realize they are drowning before they will ever call out for help or grab ahold of the life preserver that has been extended to them, the first step to salvation is for you to recognize that you are a sinner in need of salvation. You also need to realize that you are utterly incapable of saving yourself. (Read Romans 3:23, 5:8-9, Luke 19:10)

2– **Repent** The next step is to repent or turn from your sins and turn to God for forgiveness. The Scriptures declare that unless we repent, we will all likewise perish. (Read Mark 1:15, Romans 2:4, 2 Corinthians 7:10)

3– **Respond** Your response to God's call and His gift of righteousness and eternal life is to call on the Lord by faith, confess with your mouth that Jesus is Lord, and believe in your heart that God raised Him from the dead. (Read Romans 6:23, 10:9-13, Revelation 3:20)

4– **Receive** You can then receive Jesus into your heart, as well as surrender and submit to Him as your Lord and Savior. Then ask God to receive the Holy Spirit that seals you until the day of redemption. (Read John 1:12, Luke 11:13, Colossians 2:6)

If this is something that you have never done, or after reading all this now realize you need to do, then I am going to ask you to pray the following prayer from your heart:

Heavenly Father,

I confess that I have sinned against You with my words, thoughts, and actions and I recognize that my sins have separated me from You. I repent, which means I turn from my sins and ask for Your forgiveness. I believe that Jesus, being God, paid the penalty for ALL my sins when He died on the cross and rose from the dead. I ask You Jesus, to come into my life and be my Lord and my Savior. Change me from the inside out and fill me with the Holy Spirit so I can be who You called and created me to be. Thank You Jesus, for loving me, forgiving me, and for blessing me with the gift of eternal life. From this day forward I will follow You and my life is Yours.

I pray this prayer in Jesus' name, AMEN!

If you have just prayed this prayer to receive Jesus into your heart, accepted His gift of righteousness, and have trusted Him alone for your salvation, then you have just become a child of God through faith in Christ! The Scriptures declare that Heaven is rejoicing right now over your decision! Keep reading, as these last couple of chapters are going to give you some real insight and encouragement on who you are in Christ, the benefits you now have access to, and how you can walk in victory each and every day of your life!

Did you see yourself in any of the statistics at the start of this chapter?

If so, are you sure that you are really saved and born again?

For many of you reading this, Jesus is standing at the door of your heart and knocking. Whether it is to finally surrender your life to Him for the first time or it is to get back on the path you were once walking and recommit your life to Him. If you ever want to truly experience the life that you are meant to live, it can all start today. Will you take that bold step of faith and call out to God? Remember while there isn't anything that you can do that is good enough to earn His love, there also isn't anything that you have done that is bad enough to erase His love either!

BILL OF RIGHTEOUSNESS

For Christ is the end of the law
for righteousness to everyone who believes.
Romans 10:4 NKJV

M ost people know that when you are born in the United States or become a citizen of this country that you are immediately covered under the Bill of Rights. In America usage of the term *Bill of Rights* ordinarily refers to the first ten amendments of the U.S. Constitution that was ratified by the last of the necessary states in December of 1791.[1] This was done just eight years after the formal end of the Revolution in an effort to limit the powers of government in such a manner to safeguard the personal rights of its citizens.[2] The Bill of Rights is basically a formal summary of the rights, liberties, privileges, and protections guaranteed to each citizen of this country. Sadly, like the Ten Commandments, many today cannot even name the ten amendments covered under the Bill of Rights. Except for possibly freedom of speech or the right to bear arms. I guess if you've watched any court room dramas, congressional hearings, or had any run-ins with the law yourself, then you probably know what it means to "plead the Fifth" (the Fifth amendment or Article V declares that no person should be twice placed in jeopardy of life or limb, nor be compelled in a criminal case to be a witness against himself). Yeah, if that last one hit a little too close to home, you know the deal by now, just keep looking straight ahead and no one will ever know.

Hopefully, after last chapter you are now right with God through the precious blood of Jesus[3] and are a Spirit-filled,[4] born again,[5] follower of Christ[6] whose name is written in the Lamb's Book of Life.[7] If so, there are some really amazing things that you need to know that you now have access to.

Despite the negative commentary that I am sure we all hear on a daily basis from people living in this country, when you are born in or become a citizen of the United States of America it automatically comes with some inherent blessings, rights, benefits, and protections. Same is true when you are born again into the Kingdom of God. You instantly have some rights, liberties, privileges, and protections that you are blessed with as a citizen of Heaven.[8] So, these next couple pages, I want to spend a little time talking about what righteousness is and isn't, and all the amazing benefits and blessings you now have access to under God's "**Bill of Righteousness**".

GIFT OF RIGHTEOUSNESS

For if by the one man's offense death reigned through the one, much more those who receive abundance of grace and of the gift of righteousness will reign in life through the One, Jesus Christ. Therefore, as through one man's offense judgment came to all men, resulting in condemnation, even so through one Man's righteous act the free gift came to all men, resulting in justification of life. For as by one man's disobedience many were made sinners, so also by one Man's obedience many will be made righteous.
Romans 5:17-19 NKJV

This verse really puts a smile on my face every time I read it. The first thing we need to know about righteousness is that it's a <u>GIFT</u>! That means it's not a product of doing good stuff, although being declared righteous by God will produce that kind of fruit in your life. Secondly, as someone that has been in a courtroom full of people as my charges were read, I know all too well just how shameful having all my unrighteousness exposed can be. Not to mention how having to stand before a judge who is about to render a verdict and sentence, knowing that I was guilty and deserving of whatever punishment the judge deemed right, is a terribly helpless feeling as well.

Now picture that same scenario, only this time the courtroom is filled with a heavenly host of saints. The prosecuting attorney is the devil, who is passionately proclaiming the long list of all the sins, transgressions, and iniquities that I have ever committed in my life to the Judge who is Almighty God! Just as my eternal verdict is about to be handed down, the Son of God rises in the courtroom and presents His precious blood as payment in full for my offenses. I fall to my knees with tears streaming down my face as the Creator of the Universe announces that ALL my charges have been dismissed and declares me to be righteous and justified!

Hard to comprehend, isn't it? But that is a really accurate depiction of what takes place the moment we truly surrender our lives to Jesus as our Lord and Savior. I say that because the word *justification* or *justified* is a legal term that is used regarding a favorable verdict. It's from the Greek word *dikaiosis*[9] or *dikaioo*[10] which means to absolve, acquit, clear from any charge, render just or innocent, and to declare righteous. A simpler way of putting it is in God's eyes justified means "just as if I" had never sinned!!

As unbelievable as that sounds, God doesn't just stop there. He goes on to declare that those who receive the abundance of grace and the "gift of righteousness" will **REIGN** in life.[11] Starting to understand why I took the time to address all those spiritual things? See it doesn't matter how much worldly success you may experience in this life, if at the end of it all you are not right with God. In fact, the Scriptures declare this very point by proclaiming, "For what profit is it to a man if he gains the whole world, and loses his own soul?[12]

You will never truly be able to live up to your full God-given potential and experience the abundant life that God has promised to you while you are still carrying around all that guilt, shame, and condemnation that we all carry around from a life of sin. That is why you must be born again and declared righteous by your Heavenly Father. Then and only then can you reign in life and become the person you were created to be, and quite honestly have secretly longed to be!

AWAKE TO RIGHTEOUSNESS!

> *Awake to righteousness, and do not sin;*
> *for some do not have the knowledge of God.*
> *I speak this to your shame.*
> 1 Corinthians 15:34 NKJV

Have you ever experienced any devastating consequences as a result of sin, whether it was yours or another's? Stuff like divorce, depression, debt, disease, death, despair? I know one of the most devastating aspects of sin, is not only what it takes from you (peace of mind, your good name, right standing with God... to name just a few), but what it leaves you with (like guilt, shame, remorse, regret, and condemnation).

That is why as born again, Spirit-filled, new creations, one of the first things we need to do is to "awake to righteousness". In fact, the Scriptures go on to say, "And do this, knowing the time, that now it is high time to **awake out of sleep**; for now our salvation is nearer than when we first believed. The night is far spent, the day is at hand. Therefore let us cast off the works of darkness, and let us put on the armor of light. Let us walk properly, as in the day, not in revelry and drunkenness, not in lewdness and lust, not in strife and envy. But put on the Lord Jesus Christ, and make no provision for the flesh, to fulfill its lusts."[13]

So in other words, take God at His Word, quit making excuses for your sinful behavior, and start living life as the person that God created you to be in true righteousness and true holiness.[14]

That means to stop seeing yourself, and even speaking about yourself as this worthless, wretched ungodly sinner, but instead see yourself as God sees you, as a chosen generation, a royal priesthood, a holy nation.[15] God's own special people, a saint,[16] sanctified[17] and redeemed in the Lord,[18] accepted in the Beloved,[19] highly favored[20] and clothed in Christ's righteousness.[21]

I grew up Catholic, so I know that "saint" part can be hard for many of us to wrap our minds around. As many grew up believing that a saint is someone in a movie or on a medallion that was martyred for their faith and has a statue built after them; but that is not Biblical. If you look at the majority of the Apostle Paul's letters to the churches, he doesn't address them as to the sinners at Ephesus, Philippi or Colossae, but to the SAINTS.[22]

The moment you surrender your life to God and receive Jesus as your personal Lord and Savior you immediately go from being a sinner to being a Saint! Now, that doesn't mean there isn't still a sanctification and maturing process that needs to take place, during which we are conformed into the image of His Son[23] (remember the sculptor and elephant stories in Chapter 13 *Put Off, Put On, And Put Away*). So even though we are not holy or righteous at the moment of conversion, we stand in relation to God as though we were. That is because God declares the end from the beginning,[24] and as His children, He no longer sees our unrighteousness, but instead sees Christ's righteousness.[25] That is why if you ever want to be who God called you to be and do what God has called you to do then you need to **"Awake to Righteousness!"**

BENEFITS OF RIGHTEOUSNESS

> *Bless the Lord, O my soul, And forget not all*
> *His benefits: Who forgives all your iniquities,*
> *Who heals all your diseases, Who redeems your*
> *life from destruction, Who crowns you with*
> *lovingkindness and tender mercies, Who satisfies*
> *your mouth with good things, So that your youth*
> *is renewed like the eagle's.*
> Psalm 103:2-5 NKJV

Have you ever worked for a company that had some good benefits? Maybe you have even gotten a certain credit card, cable package, or life insurance policy simply because of the benefits they offered you. I am sure we can all agree that there are definitely some benefits to being born into a wealthy family or even having a father who is famous or royalty. So why do we think it is any different being born again into a heavenly family? A family where our Father is the King of Kings,[26] and all creation declares His Majesty.[27] In fact, He is so rich that His city is pure gold,[28] the walls of His city are adorned with all kinds of precious stones[29] and even the streets of His city are pure gold, like transparent glass.[30] Plus, His house has many mansions that are prepared for His children[31] and His kingdom is an eternal kingdom where there is no more death, sorrow, crying, or pain.[32]

A few years back I had an aunt that I never really knew, who died and left me and my sister part of her inheritance. Fortunately, for me someone from my mom's side of the family tracked me down and let me know about her passing and that she had left me a little something in her will. I am sure some of you that are reading this are completely unaware of the Will and Testament of Jesus Christ[33] and what He has left for each of us as His children.[34] See, many mistakenly believe that God's benefits are only available when this life ends, but in all actuality, they begin the very moment that He exchanges our sins for His righteousness. Let's pause and take a look at some of the amazing benefits that are available for us **right now** having been clothed in His righteousness:

1– He blesses the home of the righteous. Proverbs 3:33 ESV

2– He layeth up sound wisdom for the righteous. Proverbs 2:7

3– Righteousness delivers from death. Proverbs 10:2 NKJV

4– No grave trouble will overtake the righteous. Proverbs 12:21 NKJV

5– The wealth of the sinner is stored up for the righteous. Proverbs 13:22 NKJV

6– The desire of the righteous will be granted. Proverbs 10:24 NKJV

7– The righteous are bold as a lion. Proverbs 28:1 NKJV

8– The righteous who walks in his integrity-blessed are his children after him! Proverbs 20:7 ESV

9– The righteous is delivered out of trouble. Proverbs 11:8

10- The offspring of the righteous will be delivered.
   Proverbs 11:21 ESV

11- The righteous will flourish like a green leaf. Proverbs 11:28 ESV

12- The fruit of the righteous is a tree of life. Proverbs 11:30 ESV

13- In the house of the righteous there is much treasure.
   Proverbs 15:6 ESV

14- He hears the prayer of the righteous. Proverbs 15:29 NKJV

15- The Lord upholds the righteous. Psalm 37:17 NKJV

16- I have not seen the righteous forsaken or his children begging
   for bread. Psalm 37:25 ESV

17- The righteous shall inherit the land and dwell upon it forever.
   Psalm 37:29 ESV

18- The prayer of a righteous person has great power as it is working.
   James 5:16 ESV

19- When the righteous are in authority, the people rejoice.
   Proverbs 29:2 NKJV

20- The righteous will shine forth as the sun in the kingdom of their
   Father. Matthew 13:43 NKJV

21- The eyes of the Lord are on the righteous, And His ears are open
   to their prayers. 1 Peter 3:12 NKJV

Those are just a few of the blessings and benefits that come from having right standing with our Heavenly Father. I am also leaving you with a little reminder that I made up for myself as to what the *breastplate of RIGHTEOUSNESS* that God has given each of us stands for. Hope you like it:

R *est* in Christ. Matthew 11:28-29

I *nherit* the promises. Hebrews 6:12

G *ifted* spiritually. Ephesians 4:7-8

H *oly Spirit*-filled. Acts 2:4

T *reasure* in earthen vessel. 2 Corinthians 4:7

E *quipped* for every good work. 2 Timothy 3:17

O *vercoming* power. Revelation 12:11

U *nity* in Christ. Ephesians 4:13

S *aints/sons/shining lights,* no longer sinners/strangers. John 1:12, Philippians 2:15, 1 Corinthians 1:2

N *ew* creations, all things new. 2 Corinthians 5:17

E *ternal* security. 2 Corinthians 5:1

S *trong* in the Lord. Ephesians 6:10

S *ealed* with the Holy Spirit. Ephesians 1:13

Have you been "sleeping" on the blessings, benefits, privileges, and protections God has provided for you as a born again believer?

How does the knowledge of how God sees you change the way you see yourself?

Will you wake up each morning and declare that you are the righteousness of God in Christ Jesus and begin claiming the promises that God has for you and your household?

If you are currently facing a temptation or trial in your life, pick one or two of the promises God gives to the righteous and try adding them to your prayers this week. For example, if you are facing a financial crisis remind God of His promise that the wealth of the wicked is stored up for the righteous, and that God also promised to never forsake the righteous or have his children begging for bread!

CHAPTER 16

THE KEYS TO VICTORY

But thanks be to God, who gives us
the victory through our Lord Jesus Christ.
1 Corinthians 15:57 NKJV

Do you know that God is so amazing that He gives us strength for struggles we haven't faced yet,[1] healing for sicknesses we haven't felt yet,[2] and even victory for battles we haven't fought yet.[3] Our job as believers is just to walk in the strength, healing, and victory that God has already provided.

I'm sure some of you are probably thinking, why in the world with a book that has the title *Putting Away Childish Things (PACT) Keys To Unlock Your God-Given Potential*, did I make you wait until Chapter 16 to give you the keys? Good question. In my defense the answer is similar to the reason why I wouldn't just give my teenage son the keys to my new car when he asked for them. He wasn't ready for them yet! I knew that there were some things we needed to cover first before he could responsibly handle those keys. Sorry to say this, but same is true for those of you reading this. There were some things we needed to work out and go over before you were actually ready to be handed these keys.

Besides, in this instant everything, touch screen, hi-speed internet world that we live in today, had I just given you "the keys" right from the start, many of you may not have even read the other chapters of the book! Am I lying? Again, I'm sorry but I'm just keeping it real.

I'm sure I'm not the only one that has ever "misplaced" (aka lost) their keys, right? You search all over for those things and then just when you are about to lose it, you find them in the least likely spot imaginable. Like the refrigerator, dirty clothes hamper, under the bed, or the ignition of your car. I say that because the keys I am about to hand you have been just sitting in a spot you probably wouldn't ever think to look, which is in the Bible.

PACT KEY 1- MEDITATE ON GOD'S WORD

This Book of the Law shall not depart
from your mouth, but you shall meditate
on it day and night, so that you may be careful
to do according to all that is written in it. For
then you will make your way prosperous,
and then you will have good success.
Joshua 1:8 ESV

One of the childish things I always used to struggle with was procrastination. Especially when it came to doing my homework or studying for a big test. I would play, watch television, and do just about anything else to put off what I knew I was supposed to be doing. Then I would try to cram a week's worth of information into a couple of frantic minutes, probably why I did not do so well in school and would always have to take the test over. Sadly, many people are the same way when it comes to reading their Bibles. All the while not thinking about the big test that is coming up, that they are not prepared for.

Let me ask you something, do you want to make your way prosperous? Do you want to have good success in your life? Those probably seem like silly questions, but considering all we have covered so far, I had to ask. I would hope by now the answer would be DEFINITELY *YES* to both of those questions, especially considering you picked up this book and have read 16 chapters. Here's the real question though, have you read your Bible recently and if so, are you meditating on it and being careful to do what it says? Not so much, huh? And we wonder why everything isn't working right in our lives.

This reminds me of my dad at Christmas time. I was that kid that would always want the toy that would have "assembly required" marked on it. Some of you know what I am talking about. My dad would always end up being the one trying to put this thing together for me. Problem was he would never look at the instruction manual that came with it. So when he was finished, my bike or whatever it was that year, would always have some "extra parts" laying around and would never work right. Same is true for our lives when we try to have success or prosperity, but never really bother to look at God's instruction manual, the Bible when we are putting our lives together.

To help those of you that may not know where to begin, I suggest you just start reading a chapter or two in the Gospels and then read through the New Testament. Or you can read a chapter of each the Proverbs and the Psalms every day and you will have the whole book of Proverbs completed in a month. You can even get one of those "read the Bible in a year" plans, which for most readers will only require a twenty to thirty minute commitment each day.

And for those of you who have trouble reading, there are always audio versions of the Bible, which is also effective as the Scriptures say that "faith comes by hearing, and hearing by the word of God."[4] Whatever plan you decide, I want to give you an easy method to employ with any of the passages of Scripture that you read or listen to. That way you are not just reading but applying God's Word to your life. It is called

STEPS, which is just a subtle reminder to look for the following whenever you read a portion of Scripture:

S *in* to confess
T *ruth* to believe
E *xample* to follow (or avoid)
P *romise* to stand on
S *omething* to thank God for

The Bible is not some ancient, out of touch book written to a people that have long since passed away. Instead, it is **alive and active**,[5] full of warnings,[6] wisdom,[7] counsel,[8] correction,[9] hope,[10] healing,[11] instruction,[12] and inspiration[13] for everyday living! It is not a word once spoken, but instead is a Word that is **still speaking**! Even if you have read through the Bible during your life, you are never finished reading the Bible, or having it read you!

If you ever want to truly reach your full potential and live the life you have been longing for, God gives you a simple, two-step plan. Not only on how to achieve that goal, but that puts all of those "self-help" manuals promising "7 steps to a great life" to shame. Step 1- Simply read God's Word and meditate on it. Step 2- Be vigilant to do what it says. OR, you can just keep taking the tests over and over and over again.

PACT KEY 2- PRAYER

> *Pray without ceasing.*
> 1 Thessalonians 5:17 NKJV

So how would you describe your prayer life these days? Is it vibrant, fulfilling, passionate, and fruitful? Or is it dull, forced, uninspired and lifeless? Basically, something you memorized as a kid with a couple of quick **"bless"** and **"be withs"** thrown in for good measure. I think for many, the truth is more of the latter, right? This is probably due to one of two things. First, you have bought into the lie of religion that prayer is some boring routine or ritual[14] that believers must force themselves to do every day to stay right with God. This is a persuasive lie that I hope I helped expose in the previous Chapter 15 *Bill of Righteousness*. Our right standing with God is never based on our good works, but on Christ's finished work on the cross. Besides let us never lose sight that prayer shouldn't be like some childhood chore that we've "got to do", but rather it is a privilege and an honor that we "GET TO DO." Think about it, like Adam in the garden we get to walk and talk each day with our God, Creator, and Heavenly Father![15]

The second thing that can hinder our prayer life, is when we lift some situation or individual in prayer and nothing seems to change or things just get worse, remember Mary and Martha's brother Lazarus in Chapter 7 *Even Now (Roll Back The Stone)*. What often happens next is that we get discouraged and eventually just stop praying. Sound familiar? I know I have been there a couple times as the *Broken Hopes and Dreams* poem I shared with you in Chapter 13 *Put Off, Put On, And Put Away* will testify to. Even though prayer may not immediately change all things in your life, it does immediately change you for all things you will face in life. Which is really the point. God is under no obligation to do what we want, but only what is right. Since He sees all and paints on a canvas too big for us to comprehend, we can trust that His timing is perfect in all things, even in answering our prayers.

The Scripture says, "Pray without ceasing".[16] I can hear some of you already, "Are you kidding me brother Mike, I've got work to do, kids to raise, bills to pay, TV shows to watch, and a life to live." Calm down, when the Apostle Paul wrote this, he didn't mean to pray non-stop, 24 hours a day. Though Jesus, at His greatest hour of need, chastised His disciples for not being able to pray for even one hour with Him.[17]

Paul was writing to the church at Thessalonica, reminding them that praying without ceasing meant making God a part of every aspect of their lives, through prayer and not just during emergencies. This is because there are a lot of things we can do after we pray, but there really should not be much of anything that we do **until we pray**. Especially when it comes to making potentially life-altering decisions. Wouldn't you rather have God's blessing and approval before doing something, rather than just doing it and hoping God blesses or approves of what you are doing? Exactly.

So rather than going through the motions or wrongly thinking that if you pray a certain way or on a certain day, then God has to do what you say, I want to take a moment and give you a few

Scriptural Words of encouragement on **how to strengthen your prayer life**, if that's alright?

- Center prayers on the worship of God– Luke 11:1-2, Psalm 150:6
- Focus prayers on the face of God (not just His hand)– 2 Chronicles 7:14, Psalm 27:7-8
- Pray prayers inspired by the Spirit of God– Romans 8:26-27, John 16:13
- Pray prayers offered thru the Son of God– John 16:23-24, Acts 3:6

In addition, to keep your prayer life from becoming unfruitful or frustrating, I'm going to give you some reasons God lists in His Word on why prayers **aren't answered**. They are as follows:

- Prayers that are outside of God's will– 1 John 5:14
- Prayers that are offered amiss (selfish reasons)– James 4:3
- Not honoring spouse in marriage– 1 Peter 3:7
- Ongoing sin in our lives– Psalm 66:18

With that being said, my best counsel is to just pray genuine, heartfelt prayers that line up with the Word of God. This is why some of the best prayers are often simply: **"God Please Help Me, Deliver Me, Heal Me, or God Please Save Me."** That is because thankfully God isn't moved by the elegance of our words, but by the sincerity of our hearts.

Important: do not get discouraged if God doesn't seem to respond immediately. Daniel in the Old Testament is a good example that there are sometimes things going on in the spiritual realm that can delay our prayers from being answered[18] (remember the poem *Broken Hopes and Dreams* in Chapter 13 *Put Off, Put On, and Put Away*).

A little saying that I have heard over the years to remind me of this is: *If I am wrong God says "GROW". If my request is wrong God says "NO". If the timing is wrong God says "SLOW," but if all three are right God says, "LET'S GO"!!* I know it is a bit corny, but it still helps me to remember that God is God, and I'm not God! That is why at the end of the day all my prayers end with, **"Not my will, but Yours be done Lord."**[19]

PACT KEY 3– GET BAPTIZED

> *Or do you not know that as many of us as were baptized into Christ Jesus were baptized into His death? Therefore we were buried with Him through baptism into death, that just as Christ was raised from the dead by the glory of the Father, even so we should walk in the newness of life.*
> Romans 6:3-4 NKJV

I remember when I was about six or seven, my mom and I would watch church on television each Sunday morning. Seeing those preachers deliver a passionate message and how people in the congregation would respond, really sparked something in me to do that someday. I also really loved it when they would do baptisms. So, one day I grabbed our cat and tried to baptize him in the tub. Needless to say, the cat was not too happy about that and went screeching out of the bathroom. When my mom saw this, she rushed in and asked what I was doing? I said, "I am trying to baptize the cat so it can go to Heaven one day." She in no uncertain terms told me that, "You can't baptize a cat," to which I responded, "Well he shouldn't have joined my church then!"

There are many types and shadows of baptism throughout the Old Testament, such as Noah and his family in the ark,[20] Moses and the Israelites crossing the Red Sea,[21] and even the Jewish ceremonial cleansing prescribed in both Leviticus[22] and Exodus.[23] But the New Testament church is told to repent and be **baptized**,[24] believe and be **baptized**,[25] and the *Great Commission* which Jesus, left us with, "Go therefore and make disciples of all nations, **baptizing** them in the name of the Father and of the Son and of the Holy Spirit."[26]

The word baptism comes from the Greek verb *baptizo*[27] which means to dip, immerse, or submerge. The Apostle Paul uses the common experience of believers being baptized as a picture of being identified with Jesus Christ. Baptism expresses faith the way a word expresses an idea. It is an outward expression of an inward transformation. Water baptism signifies purification, initiation, and identification with Christ. Just as a cloth dipped in dye absorbs the color of the dye, so a person fully immersed in Christ should take on the nature of Christ.

So, baptism is a symbol of the spiritual union of Christ and the believer. When a person trusts Christ, he or she is incorporated and united to Jesus Christ, which includes being united to His death. Jesus' death becomes our death. It also stands to reason that if the believer identifies with His death, then we should also identify with His resurrection. Therefore, having died and having been raised with Christ, the believer should live a new kind of life.[28] This is essential to being who God intended you to be, which in turn will lead to living your best and blessed life.

PACT KEY 4– GO TO CHURCH

Not forsaking the assembling of
ourselves together, as is the manner of some,
but exhorting one another, and so much
the more as you see the Day approaching.
Hebrews 10:25 NKJV

Seems to me a lot of people approach church like a mouse approaches a mousetrap. By that I mean, they want to get something, without getting "caught". I have found that when you ask most people why they do not go to church anymore, a few say, "Yeah I know I need to start going again" or "Man, I'm just so busy right now, I don't have the time." But most people I have found will say, "Oh those Christians are all just a bunch of self-righteous, Bible thumping phonies and hypocrites, so I stopped going." I am sure some of you reading this have heard something along those lines before or maybe even said something like that before about Christians and churchgoers.

The thing is while there is no doubt that there are many self-righteous phonies and hypocrites in churches all over the world, my follow up question to them is always, "What does any of that have to do with you going to church?" There are fakes, phonies, and hypocrites everywhere! Go to an AA meeting (these people are trying to change but usually barely hanging on!), a sporting event (think they were wearing that jersey before the team started winning?), or just go to one of those online dating sites (I am sure everyone on there really looks like their picture!) These things don't stop you from going to the meeting, game, or online any more than all the fake knock-off diamonds, watches, or money out there stops you from desiring or seeking after the real thing.

Plus, it is always easier to point out the flaws with the church or other Christians than it is to stop and examine your own life like we did in Chapter 13 *Put Off, Put On, and Put Away.* Sadly, most people judge others by their actions, but judge themselves by their intentions (well I really didn't mean to do that). Or worse, they put others' lives under a microscope and won't even look in a mirror at themselves. I wrote a little poem about this mindset when it comes to judging the church and its members; it is called:

Perfect Church

If you could find the perfect church
without fault or fear,
For goodness' sake don't join that church
you'd spoil the atmosphere.

If you should find the perfect church
where all anxieties cease,
Then pass it by lest stepping in
you mar the masterpiece.

If you should find the perfect church
then enter don't you dare,
To step foot upon such holy ground
you'd be a misfit there.

Of course it's not a perfect church
that's simple to discern,
But you and I and all of us
could cause the tide to turn.

And since no perfect church exists
made of imperfect men,
Then let's just stop looking for that church
and love the one we're in!

I say that for anyone that has been pointing out or using the fact that the churches today have problems as an excuse for not going. Point being, even if you could find a perfect church then they probably wouldn't have you as a member. And if they did, they wouldn't be "perfect" anymore when you attended, would they? So, while God is greatly concerned with hypocrisy in the church, so much so that He gives us Biblical instructions on how to deal with it, we don't go to church for others, but for God!

By now you have probably noticed I like catchy little acronyms to help me remember stuff. Yeah, I am old like that. So, if it is alright I'm going to share one more with you that I have come up with to remind me why we are to go to church, it's **WASH**:

W *orship* God
A *cknowledge* God
S *erve* God
H *ear* (from) God

If you really want to know how church is supposed to function, I encourage you to read the book of Acts, especially Acts 2:40-47. When you look at how the early church operated, you will be blown away. When they prayed, there was power. When they spoke, there was authority. When they embraced, there was love. And when they gave, there was generosity. So much so that the Scriptures say that they "sold their possessions and goods, and divided them among all, as anyone had need."[29] Can you picture churches today operating like that? But that's the way God designed the church to be, and Jesus is coming back for a church without spot or blemish,[30] we all need to quit "playing church" and get back to practicing real Christian values as a church. It can start with you deciding to not only be a church goer, but a church grower!

PACT KEY 5– FELLOWSHIP WITH OTHER CHRISTIANS

But if we walk in the light, as He is in the light, we
have fellowship with one another, and the blood
of Jesus Christ his Son cleanseth us from all sin.
1 John 1:7

You are probably wondering how fellowship is a key to reaching your God-given potential. Good question, glad you asked. For starters the word fellowship is from the Greek word *koinonia*,[31] which means communion, partnership, or that which is shared in common. That is important because God didn't design and create you to be alone.

The Bible really illustrates this point as it says:

Two are better than one because they have a good
return for their labor; for if either of them falls, the one
will lift up his companion. But woe to the one who falls
when there is not another to lift him up! Furthermore,
if two lie down together they keep warm, but how
can one be warm alone? And if one can overpower
him who is alone, two can resist him. A cord of three
strands is not quickly torn apart.
Ecclesiastes 4:9-12 NASB

Pretty powerful visual, huh? Also a big reason Jesus sent His disciples out two by two.[32] Really all that just confirms is what we already know to be true, which is that we all need help from time to time. Especially in doing what God has called us to do and getting to where God wants to get us. Even Jesus needed help carrying his cross;[33] think you will not need some help carrying yours?

Another thing genuine fellowship provides is support, encouragement, and accountability. Something I know I desperately need in my life, especially the accountability, as we have already established in previous chapters, every way we do things is right in our own eyes.[34] Plus, just as we all have blind spots in our cars, we have them in our lives as well. So, if you want to walk fast, go ahead and continue to walk alone. But if you want to walk far and fulfill your God-given purpose, then you are going to need to walk with others.

PACT KEY 6– BE A BOLD WITNESS FOR CHRIST

But you shall receive power when the
Holy Spirit has come upon you; and you shall be
witnesses to Me in Jerusalem, and in all Judea and
Samaria, and to the end of the earth.
Acts 1:8 NKJV

We all know that eyewitness testimony in a case is some of the most powerful and convincing evidence that can be offered. So why is it that so many of us struggle to share our faith or be a bold witness for Jesus? The answer is simple; we are afraid that someone will raise an objection or ask a question that we don't have an answer to, right? So, let's look at that for a moment. The word *witness* is from the Greek word *martus*[35] which is where we get the word Martyr. That is not only someone whose death bears witness to the truth, but someone who testifies to the truth no matter what the cost or consequences.[36]

It is no different than being called to the witness stand in a courtroom. You do not need to know **everything** in order to offer up testimony, right? Same is true with being a Christian witness. You just need to be willing to stand up for your faith and bear witness to what you have seen, heard, or know to be true about Jesus. While people will often argue about who Jesus is or the reliability of the Scriptures, there really is no refuting what you tell them that you have seen the Lord do in your life or in the lives of those around you. I can say this because I have personally been healed by Jesus. I've also personally experienced God deliver me from drugs and alcohol (I have been clean and sober for over 30 years now). I have personally witnessed God doing miraculous things in other people's lives as well and if that is not incredible enough, I have actually been told I was going to die from cancer, only to have God spare me, deliver me, and give me life!

Besides, our call as Christians is not to convince others that the Bible is true or that God is real, but rather to, "Not be ashamed of the testimony of our Lord;"[37] to "Go into all the world and preach the gospel to every creature;"[38] to be a living epistle which is known and read by all men;[39] and to always be ready to give an answer to everyone who asks you a reason for the hope that is in you, with meekness and fear.[40]

Thing is when we witness, share our faith, or even our testimony with another person, one of three things can happen: 1– The person receives Jesus and transforms their life;[41] 2– A seed is planted (or watered) in the person's heart;[42] 3– They completely reject what you are saying to them about Jesus, in which case the Scriptures say to "Rejoice in that day and leap for joy! For indeed your reward is great in heaven."[43]

I do not know about you, but that sounds like a WIN-WIN-WIN scenario to me!! If that's not motivation enough, Jesus says that if you confess Him before men, that He will confess you before His Father. On the other hand, He also says that if you deny Him before men, then He will deny you before His Father who is in Heaven.[44]

In closing:

When things get tough or you feel like giving up, always remember things that seem impossible with men are possible with God.[45] And my favorite Scripture... that YOU <u>CAN DO</u> **ALL** THINGS THROUGH CHRIST WHO STRENGTHENS YOU.[46]

God has given you the keys; will you use them to unlock the power, promises, and passageway to your God-given potential?

To bring the importance of having the right keys full circle, I want to share a little story. I'm sure all of us have watched some version of the movie Titanic. Pretty much only need to watch it once as it always turns out the same, right? What you may not know is that the night before Titanic was to take off on it's tragic journey, Second Officer David Blair was replaced by Charles Tolliver. Seemingly insignificant detail, unless of course if you were David Blair, who was likely spared from a watery grave. The thing most don't realize is that after the Titanic departed, David Blair realized he had a very important key still in his pocket. It was a key to a small locker in the crow's nest of the ship that held a pair of special binoculars. You have to be mindful that we are talking pre-sonar era and these special binoculars would enable a person in the crow's nest to see obstacles in the water that they couldn't see with the natural eye, thus averting disaster.

My point being not only do you need the keys to unlock the spiritual binoculars God designed for you to see obstacles long before they shipwreck your life. But also, God is asking you to pass those same keys on to those coming after you so they can see and avoid the potential life altering danger that lies beyond their ability to see with their natural eyes. Hopefully this short little piece of history will help bring home the importance of not only having the keys, but passing them on, amen?

Now that you have been given the **PACT Keys** to living a blessed and abundant life, what will you do with them? Start unlocking your God given potential, share them with others, or just set them back on the shelf?

Which key do you believe will be the most challenging for you to use:

- Meditating on God's Word
- Prayer
- Getting baptized
- Going to church
- Fellowshipping with other Christians
- Being a bold witness for Christ

I know if you've been doing your homework then you probably have a ton of stuff taped to your mirror already (your vision/life goals, **SMART Plan** for achieving those goals, mission statement, etc.), but I'm going to ask you to add the list of the keys to your mirror as well, in order of hardest to easiest, and then make a commitment right now to put that key that is the most challenging into practice every day for the next forty days, until you have it mastered. Will you do that?

CHAPTER 17

NEW YOU RESOLUTION!

God can do more thru 1 person who is
100% committed to Him, than He can thru
100 people who are 90% committed.
Dr. Robert J. Clinton

How many resolutions have you made in your life, especially around New Year's? You know the ones that usually start with "This year **I'm going to stop** _____ (eating junk food, cussing, partying so much, etc.) and **I'm going to start** _____ (exercising, dieting, spending more time with the kids, going to church, etc.) There may even be a few of you reading this that have made those declarations, pleas, promises, or resolutions to God in a moment of desperation. They usually sound more like "God if you help me (get me out of this, make this room quit spinning, etc.) **then I promise to** _____ (stop drinking, treat others better, never do that again, or even surrender my life to you!). Any of those sound familiar? I thought they might.

Now here is the real question. How many of those resolutions, declarations, pleas, or promises that you made with God are you still sticking to or honoring? Not so many if any, huh? For the record, the word **_resolution_** or **_resolute_** in the Webster's dictionary means the following:

1– Firm determination.

2– A course of action determined or decided on.

3– An act of resolving to do something.

4– A formal statement of a decision or expression of opinion adopted by an assembly such as the U.S. Congress.

5– Marked by firmness or determination; unwavering

I am sure we all meant what we said at the time. We had a "firm determination" and had seriously "resolved" that we really wanted to make those changes in our life, correct? I know I did. So, what happened? Well, for me usually the crisis would die down, then my resolve would slowly fade and eventually I would just end up getting discouraged and going back to doing what I had always done. I am sure many are nodding their heads in agreement. If it is alright with you, I want to spend a little time talking about how we can really make lasting change in our lives.

Partakers of the divine nature

> As His divine power has given to us all things
> that pertain to life and godliness, through the
> knowledge of Him who called us by glory and
> virtue, by which have been given to us
> exceedingly great and precious promises,
> that through these you may be partakers
> of the divine nature, having escaped the corruption
> that is in the world through lust. But also
> for this very reason, giving all diligence, add to
> your faith virtue, to virtue knowledge, to knowledge

self-control, to self-control perseverance, to perseverance
godliness, to godliness brotherly kindness,
and to brotherly kindness love. For if these things
are yours and abound, you will be neither barren
nor unfruitful in the knowledge of our Lord Jesus
Christ. For he who lacks these things is shortsighted,
even to blindness, and has forgotten
that he was cleansed from his old sins.
Therefore, brethren, be even more diligent
to make your call and election sure, for if you
do these things you will never stumble.
2 Peter 1:3 10 NKJV

I know there is a lot to take in with that Scripture, but it is just over-flowing with good stuff, so please bear with me. I am sure most of you have probably heard the story of the frog and the scorpion. If not let me give you a quick recap.

Basically, a scorpion comes to a large body of water that he has no way of getting across. The scorpion then sees a frog and asks him to give him a ride on his back across the exceptionally large pond. The frog naturally is hesitant, telling the scorpion, "No, you'll sting me and I'll die!" After repeatedly promising not to sting him, the scorpion eventually convinces the frog to take him across. About halfway across the pond the scorpion suddenly stings the frog. The frog, as he is dying, looks back at the scorpion and asks, "Why did you do that; you've killed us both?!" The scorpion's simple reply, "Sorry, it's my nature."

The point of the story and the reason we have struggled so much in the past to change is simply because it was *our old, sinful nature* that caused us to keep messing up and doing the same stuff.

That is why this passage is such good news. Essentially, it tells us that as Spirit-filled,[1] born again,[2] new creations[3] and followers of Jesus.[4] We are *partakers*, which means we are participants who get to have a share or portion of a specified quality or characteristic.[5] Which in this case is the *divine nature*. So, all that time I spent trying, crying, praying, and promising to change the things I was doing, God was just waiting for me to surrender. He knew once He changed me, then over time that inward change that He began inside my heart, would be the key to changing what I did and how I was living outwardly.

But God in His infinite wisdom, knew that there would still occasionally be times in our walk when we would give place to the devil.[6] Who by the way, just loves to remind us of who we were and that in turn leads us to forget that we have been cleansed from our former sins. Which, like those electric clocks that get disconnected from their power source and end up going back into "default mode" (blinking 12:00), can lead us to reverting to some of our old default mode, sinful ways. The good news is that all we have to do is run back to God and reconnect to our ultimate power source, the Holy Spirit.[7] This is the only way we can ever hope to achieve victory over sin and lasting change in our lives. Does that make sense? If so, can I get an amen?

THE "GOLDEN RULE"

> *Therefore, whatever you want*
> *men to do to you, do also to them,*
> *for this is the Law and the Prophets.*
> Matthew 7:12 NKJV

I am not going to spend a lot of time in this section as it is pretty self-explanatory. I am sure all of us in some way, shape, or form have heard some version of the *Golden Rule*, which is basically to treat others the way you would want to be treated. When I look around at all the hatred, fighting, violence, and even indifference in the world towards people that are hurting, homeless, or even just "different" than us, it is not hard to see that we are not living by this rule so much anymore.

Just so you know, I was really close to adding this as a seventh key to unlocking your God-given potential, but decided against it, as this is more of a command and overall core principle we should all strive to live by and adhere to each and every day. So, I just took some time to write out some biblical ways, that not only I would like to be treated, but more importantly how God says to treat others; or in this case "one another." I hope they encourage and light a fire in you like they have with me:

"ONE ANOTHERS" IN THE SCRIPTURES

1– Love **one another** with brotherly affection. Outdo **one another** in showing honor. Romans 12:10 ESV

2– Live in harmony with **one another.** Romans 12:16 ESV

3– Welcome **one another** as Christ has welcomed you. Romans 15:7 ESV

4– Be kind to **one another**, tenderhearted, forgiving **one another**, as God in Christ forgave you. Ephesians 4:32 ESV

5– Through love serve **one another.** Galatians 5:13 ESV

6– Encourage **one another** and build **one another.** 1 Thessalonians 5:11 ESV

7– Let us consider how to stir up **one another** to love and good works. Hebrews 10:24 ESV

8– For this is the message that you have heard from the beginning, that we should love **one another**. 1 John 3:11 ESV

9– Show hospitality to **one another** without grumbling. 1 Peter 4:9 ESV

10– Exhort **one another** daily. Hebrews 3:13

11– Confess your sins to **one another** and pray for **one another,** that you may be healed. James 5:16 ESV

12– Forbearing **one another** and forgiving **one another**, if any man have a quarrel against any; even as Christ forgave you, so also do ye. Colossians 3:13

13– A new commandment I give to you, that you love **one another**; as I have loved you, that you also love **one another**. John 13:34 NKJV

14– Submitting to **one another** in the fear of God. Ephesians 5:21 NKJV

<u>WARNING</u>

But if you bite and devour one another,
beware lest you be consumed by one another!
Galatians 5:15 NKJV

We all know the saying that hurt people, hurt people. Let's add wounded people, wound people and angry people are angry with people. But God says for forgiven people to forgive people, blessed people to bless people, and loved people to love people. Be mindful of how you treat others (or one another) today. **Is it how you would want to be treated yourself?**

GENERATIONAL "EXCHANGE ZONE"

> *And these things that you have heard from me*
> *among many witnesses, commit these to faithful*
> *men who will be able to teach others also.*
> 2 Timothy 2:2 NKJV

This may come as a surprise to some of you, but I used to be a serious runner back in the day. Hard to believe I know, but it is true. I actually finished third in the state in the half mile as a freshman, before partying, girls, and cars led me down a different path. Nowadays I just race my eight year old granddaughter Leila, who by the way beats me every time! Back then, I was a bit like *Forrest Gump*. By that I don't mean that I grew a crazy beard and ran across the country, although I did run cross-country as a freshman in high school. What I mean, is that like the Tom Hanks character in the movie, I just loved to run. Whether it was to the store, school, a friend's house, or anywhere else, chances are if you saw me as a child or even in my early teens, I was running.

The race that I loved the most though, was without a doubt the relay race! There was always just something about running against other runners with that baton in my hand, and then having to smoothly pass it off to my teammate so he could run, that was always so exciting. These days, while I may occasionally look back at the God-given potential and opportunities that I squandered as a young man, I am grateful that God has given me an eternal baton to carry and pass on to my children, grandchildren, nieces, nephews, as well as this up-and-coming generation.

The thing is though, that just like in the relay races I loved so much back in the day, there is still a limited amount of time to pass that baton to the next runner. For us as Christians that "exchange zone" is basically when the Lord comes back again or that dash in between the two dates on our tombstone. Whichever comes first. So since yesterday is gone and tomorrow is not promised, that tells me I need to live every day as if it were my last. Now when I say that I'm not saying to just go out and spend our lives recklessly, but a better way of putting it is: to live each day as if Jesus died yesterday, rose today, and is coming back tomorrow!

The great thing about it is you never really know how many generations you can impact and inspire with how you run your race and what you pass on in the exchange zone! Look at the passage above. Paul is basically coming to the end of his race[8] and is passing on that proverbial baton to a young man in the faith named Timothy. While he is passing it, you can hear him giving words of encouragement to basically *commit* (or pass on) to faithful men, who in turn will also be able to teach others.

Basically, he laid out in the passage four generations of hand-offs and exchanges from Paul to Timothy, then Timothy to faithful men, and lastly the faithful men to other men. Honestly if you read between the lines of the text, it is really a never ending, eternal exchange. That is because the recent man to get the baton (which is us), has the same charge as the first one to run with it did. Which is to pass on the godly wisdom, confidence, life experiences, and all that God has blessed you with and brought you through in your life to the next generation of believer's that are about to face the very same challenges! God has not only given you a banner to fly, a song to sing, and a message to deliver, but a baton to exchange. Even if you have dropped your baton, there is still time for you to pick it back up and pass it to the person waiting for it. Will you do it, or will you just leave the next runner hanging?

How does knowing that as a child of God you are now a partaker of the divine nature change how you see situations in your life?

Have you been following the *Golden Rule* in the way you treat others and which of the "**one anothers**" do you need to do a better job at?

What baton are you passing off to the next generation?

I am giving you a generic copy of the **PACT Resolution** (written similar to the *Courageous Resolution* for fatherhood) that I hand out at the men's conferences I minister at. Rather than just asking you to fill it out, sign it, and get it cosigned, I am going to encourage you to go a little deeper than that. I'm sure everyone has a computer or at the very least access to a computer.

If you are serious about making some changes in your life or even just stepping up and committing to being a better spouse, parent, coworker, and follower of Jesus then I want you to spend some time in prayer and the Word and come up with your own **personalized resolution** (feel free to use the one below as a template). Then get it printed off on some nice certificate paper and get it cosigned by either family, friends, brothers/sisters in Christ, or even your Pastor (that is if you are really serious).

You can probably even get a family member or two, or a couple of close friends or fellow Christians that are also looking to make some changes to step up and do a *PACT Resolution* of their own alongside of you.

Lastly, I encourage you to take this resolution seriously. Dress up and do this publicly, like at church or in front of a group of family and friends, then frame and hang your resolution up in a place of prominence in your house so that there will be accountability.

PACT RESOLUTION

I, _____, do solemnly resolve before God to put away all childish ways of talking, thinking and living. And from this day forward:

+ I will be a man of my word, of character, and of integrity.

+ I will take full responsibility for my actions and will no longer make excuses.

+ I will learn from my mistakes, repent of my sins, and walk with integrity as a man answerable to God.

+ I will confront evil, pursue justice, and love mercy.

+ I will forgive those who have wronged me and reconcile with those I have wronged.

+ I will pray for others and treat them with love, kindness, dignity, respect, and compassion.

+ I will selflessly and sacrificially love my family, protect them, serve them and teach them the Word of God as the spiritual leader of my home.

+ I will be faithful to my wife, to love and honor her, to nourish and cherish her, and be willing to lay down my life for her as Jesus Christ did for me.

+ I will bless my children and grandchildren, minister Christ to them, and be always a living model and example of His character.

+ I will boldly and courageously live an eternally minded life as I step up to be the man God has called and created me to be.

By signing this I am committing to courageously fulfill this resolution for the rest of my life.

Signature_____ Date_____

By co-signing this I am committing to encouraging and holding my brother accountable to the resolution that he made this day.

Co-Signer_____ Date_____

Co-Signer_____ Date_____

**"By the mouth of two or three witnesses
the matter shall be established."**
Deuteronomy 19:15 NKJV

EPILOGUE

Congratulations!! You made it to the end of this book! I know you probably think I am being funny or sarcastic, but I am totally serious. I also know there had to have been moments when you wanted to quit reading this and maybe even send me a really angry email, but you fought through that and finished what you started. I really do commend you for that as it is an admirable trait, especially in today's day and age where people are so quick to give up when things get tough. Although, as we have covered throughout this book, there is no easy way to any place worth going, especially when it comes to where God wants to take you.

I know this book must have challenged you in some areas of your life, as it really challenged me just writing it. But that is the point. God did not have me write this to make you comfortable. If anything, I wrote it to help get you out of your "comfort zone" so that you can be all that you were meant to be and achieve all that you were meant to achieve! I know that my approach can be direct at times, to say the least, but in my defense, I have to give it to you the way that God gives it to me.[1] Plus it really doesn't make much sense to spend a lot of time talking about how nice the wallpaper in your living room looks, when your house is on fire!

So, if you do not mind my asking, what was your favorite part of the book? How about your least favorite? Better yet, what was the hardest part of the book for you to get through? For me, the hardest chapters to write were Chapter 5 *Looking Back* and Chapter 9 *Do You Know God?*

(And Does He Know You?). As someone who grew up in a Christian household, attended Sunday school, church services and was even an altar boy, it is hard to look back at who I was and how I lived my life. Only to realize in my forties, that I was living in sin and rebellion to the God who gave me life! Who in reality I knew all about, but I never really knew. Thank God for His patience, grace and mercy!

The easiest part to write was definitely Chapter 14 *Born Again*. Even though it has been 15 years since God spoke to my heart, drew me up that isle with tears streaming down my face, and exchanged all my sin, guilt, and shame for His righteousness. That moment is forever etched in my memory and still brings tears of joy to my eyes.

I hope you liked, and even more importantly could relate to the handful of personal stories and poems I used to illustrate a spiritual truth or principle. I imagine that some of you are wondering why I did not write more about my life. Well, there will definitely come a time when I share my testimony of all God has blessed me with and brought me through, but for now I really didn't want the focus to be on the author of this book, but on the "Author and finisher of our faith,"[2] **JESUS**!

Again, I want to thank you for going on this incredible journey with me. I don't know if you know this or not, but God has placed greatness in each and every one of us. Thing is, He expects greatness out of us as well.[3] The real question is what will you do with that God-given potential?? Will you waste, disregard, or neglect the unique and amazing gifts and abilities that God has given you? Or will you wake up, grow up, show up, and step up to be the world changer, covenant keeper, and follower of Christ that you were made and meant to be?

I'd love to hear your thoughts on what you got out of this book, any impact it may have had on your life, as well as any questions you may still have. The good news is that if you keep the faith, press into God's promises, and apply the spiritual truths highlighted in this book then the best is yet to come! Remember it is not how you start, but how you finish your race that counts! May God bless you and give you strength, grace, and courage **for the rest of the journey!!**

You can reach me at mpl.pact@gmail.com

ENDNOTES

Introduction

1   1 John 2:13, 4:4
2   Romans 8:37
3   Genesis 1:26
4   Deuteronomy 28:12-13
5   Ephesians 2:10
6   Strong's 4161 (Greek)
7   Luke 13:24 NASB
8   Strong's 75 (Greek)
9   1 Peter 5:8
10   Isaiah 14:12
11   Revelation 20:10
12   Muriel Chen

Chapter 1

1   Romans 11:16
2   Genesis 3:1
3   Proverbs 22:15
4   Romans 5:19
5   Hebrews 5:8
6   John 3:3-5
7   Numbers 32:23
8   Proverbs 28:13
9   Revelation 19:8
10   Isaiah 64:6
11   Leviticus 17:11, Hebrews 9:22
12   Psalm 139:7-9
13   Revelation 20:2
14   Isaiah 14:16
15   Revelation 21:4
16   John 10:10
17   Habakkuk 2:2

Chapter 2

1   Proverbs 20:6
2   2 Corinthians 10:12
3   Luke 18:11-14
4   Romans 3:23
5   Romans 6:23
6   Isaiah 5:20
7   Luke 1:49
8   Matthew 5:28
9   1 John 3:15
10   Hebrews 9:27
11   James 2:10
12   Psalm 53:2-3
13   John 10:11
14   Psalm 84:11
15   Romans 8:28 NASB
16   Isaiah 1:19
17   Romans 2:4
18   James 1:17
19   2 Corinthians 4:4
20   2 Timothy 1:6
21   1 Timothy 4:14
22   Romans 5:17
23   Acts 2:38
24   Romans 6:23
25   1 Corinthians 12:4-11

Chapter 3

1. Colossians 2:8
2. Matthew 15:6
3. Proverbs 21:2
4. 1 John 4:8
5. Genesis 1:26
6. Genesis 2:7
7. Matthew 18:21-22
8. Strong's 266 (Greek)
9. Strong's 3900 (Greek)
10. Strong's 5771 (Hebrew)
11. James 4:17
12. Colossians 3:13
13. Matthew 6:15
14. Matthew 5:23-24, Mark 11:24-25
15. Matthew 18:23-35
16. Proverbs 21:2
17. Proverbs 14:12
18. Matthew 7:13
19. Matthew 7:14

Chapter 4

1. Proverbs 27:6
2. 1 Thessalonians 5:14
3. Proverbs 22:7
4. Proverbs 22:6
5. Deuteronomy 6:6-7
6. John 14:12
7. I Kings 2:2-3
8. Ecclesiastes 12:13
9. Micah 6:8
10. 1 Corinthians 13:11

Chapter 5

1. Genesis 3:6
2. Genesis 19:26
3. Genesis 13:10-11
4. Genesis 13:12
5. Genesis 19:1-6
6. 2 Samuel 11:2
7. Matthew 14:28-30
8. Matthew 23:16, 24
9. John 20:29
10. 2 Corinthians 4:18
11. 1 Samuel 17:34-37
12. Psalm 23:5
13. Psalm 105:37
14. 1 Kings 17:11-16
15. Luke 9:12-17, Matthew 15:32-37
16. Jonah 1:3
17. Matthew 7:24-27
18. Luke 11:24-26
19. Matthew 11:28
20. Matthew 11:29
21. Genesis 5
22. Isaiah 53:5 NKJV
23. Psalm 46:1
24. Philippians 4:19
25. Isaiah 55:11
26. Mark 11:23
27. Luke 10:19
28. Luke 11:34
29. Romans 6:23
30. Ecclesiastes 8:11
31. Romans 6:14
32. Romans 6:1-2

Chapter 6

1 John 10:10
2 Strong's 2889 (Greek)
3 Strong's 5331 (Greek)
4 2 Corinthians 4:4
5 Romans 12:2
6 John 15:19
7 1 John 2:15
8 1 John 5:19
9 1 John 2:17
10 Galatians 6:14
11 Galatians 6:8
12 Ecclesiastes 6:7
13 1 Kings 11:3
14 Ecclesiastes 4:16
15 Romans 7:16
16 Matthew 26:41
17 Philippians 3:3
18 Jeremiah 17:5
19 Galatians 5:19-21
20 Galatians 5:22-23
21 1 Peter 5:8
22 Revelation 20:2
23 Revelation 12:10
24 Revelation 9:11
25 Isaiah 14:12
26 1 Chronicles 21:1
27 Deuteronomy 13:13
28 Matthew 10:25
29 John 10:10
30 John 8:44
31 Ezekiel 28:13
32 Ezekiel 28:17
33 Job 1:11
34 Revelation 20:10
35 Edwin Cole & Winston Churchill
36 Matthew 26:28
37 Isaiah 64:6
38 John 16:33
39 Isaiah 9:6
40 Galatians 5:22
41 Strong's 7965 (Hebrew)
42 Luke 10:5, 9:5
43 Isaiah 52:7 NASB1995
44 2 Corinthians 5:7
45 Romans 1:17
46 Acts 14:9
47 Matthew 17:20
48 Ephesians 2:8
49 Hebrews 11:6
50 1 Samuel 17:10-11
51 1 Peter 5:8
52 John 10:10
53 Luke 4:1-13
54 Philippians 2:10
55 1 John 5:4-5
56 James 4:7
57 Colossians 2:14-15
58 Revelation 12:11
59 Mark 9:29
60 2 Chronicles 20:21-22
61 2 Chronicles 20:1
62 Strong's 3063 (Hebrew)
63 2 Chronicles 20:21
64 2 Chronicles 20:22
65 2 Chronicles 20:15
66 Psalm 22:3
67 1 Corinthians 15:57
68 Psalm 18:3
69 Luke 10:19
70 Romans 16:20
71 Genesis 50:20
72 Acts 28:1-5
73 Isaiah 54:17
74 Isaiah 59:19

Chapter 7

1. John 9:1-3
2. Luke 2:49
3. Romans 8:28
4. 2 Peter 3:18
5. 1 Peter 1:7
6. 2 Corinthians 1:3-4
7. Genesis 1:1
8. Matthew 10:1
9. Luke 8:52-55
10. Matthew 14:26-27
11. Mark 11:23
12. Isaiah 61:1
13. John 2:11
14. Exodus 3:14
15. Genesis 17:4
16. Genesis 18:10-14
17. Genesis 37:23-24
18. Genesis 37:28
19. Genesis 39:9-20
20. Daniel 6:10-16
21. Jonah 1
22. Daniel 3:24-27
23. Colossians 3:25
24. Luke 13:14
25. Leviticus 25:48-49
26. Leviticus 25:25
27. Ruth 4:4-6, Jeremiah 50:34
28. Exodus 6:6, Galatians 3:13
29. Ruth 4:5
30. Hebrews 4:15
31. John 11:35
32. Matthew 28:1-2
33. John 11:53
34. Galatians 3:13, 1 Corinthians 7:23
35. Luke 19:10
36. John 8:36

Chapter 8

1. 2 Kings 5:10-11
2. Matthew 9:34, 12:14, John 11:53
3. Luke 7:38-39, 15:2
4. Luke 13:14
5. Mark 2:18
6. Mark 2:23-24
7. Matthew 15:2
8. Matthew 14:25
9. Matthew 8:2-3
10. John 6:1-13
11. John 2:1-11
12. Mark 8:22-25
13. Luke 8:49-56
14. Deuteronomy 6:3
15. Exodus 3:20
16. Exodus 14:21-28
17. Exodus 2:23-25
18. Numbers 23:19
19. Mark 5:24-29
20. Mark 2:11-12
21. Matthew 14:28-29
22. Luke 5:4-6
23. Mark 5:34 NASB
24. Matthew 9:29 NKJV
25. John 10:10
26. Matthew 10:36
27. Mark 10:47
28. Mark 10:48
29. Luke 18:15 NKJV
30. Matthew 16:21-22
31. Psalm 34:19
32. 2 Timothy 3:12
33. John 16:33, Acts 14:22

Chapter 9

1. 1 Samuel 1:3
2. 1 Samuel 1:11
3. 1 Samuel 1:24-28
4. 1 Samuel 3:1
5. 1 Chronicles 28:9
6. Job 19:25 NKJV
7. Job 1:13-21
8. 1 Kings 11:1-3, Ecclesiastes 2:10-11
9. Strong's 3045 (Hebrew)
10. Genesis 4:1
11. 1 John 5:3
12. Matthew 22:37-40
13. John 13:35
14. 1 John 4:8
15. Strong's 158 (Hebrew)
16. Strong's 7474 (Hebrew)
17. Strong's 1730 (Hebrew)
18. Webster's Dictionary
19. Strong's 5368/5384 (Greek)
20. Strong's 26 (Greek)
21. Matthew 5:46
22. 1 John 4:20
23. 1 John 4:19
24. John 3:16 NKJV
25. Acts 19:14
26. Acts 19:13
27. Acts 19:15
28. Acts 19:16
29. Matthew 12:33
30. Matthew 7:18
31. Jeremiah 32:17, Matthew 19:26
32. Psalm 46:1, 139:1-10
33. Psalm 139:4, Jeremiah 1:5
34. John 10:27
35. 2 Timothy 2:19 NKJV

Chapter 10

1. John 19:35
2. Proverbs 21:2
3. Psalm 102:3
4. James 4:14
5. Romans 14:12
6. Ephesian 1:7, John 3:16-17
7. Exodus 3:13-14 NASB
8. writings of Josephus, Tacitus, & Pliny
9. John 4:25-26

Chapter 11

1. Strong's 190 (Greek)
2. Strong's 2316 (Greek)
3. Strong's 4461 (Greek)
4. Ruth 1:16-17
5. Psalm 63:8
6. John 14:1-3
7. Genesis 12:1-3, 39:3, Psalm 105:37
8. Matthew 9:9
9. Webster's Student Dictionary 2007
10. Matthew 14:16-21
11. John 6:26
12. Luke 17:13
13. Luke 17:15-19
14. John 6:60-66
15. Luke 22:33
16. Luke 22:54-62
17. John 21:1-14
18. Isaiah 1:18-19
19. 2 Timothy 3:12
20. Hebrews 12:14
21. Matthew 16:24-25
22. Revelation 19:9
23. Matthew 22:11-13
24. Strong's 3868 (Greek)

Chapter 12

1 Strong's 2588 (Greek)
2 Proverbs 21:23 NKJV
3 Proverbs 19:9 NKJV
4 Proverbs 18:21 NKJV
5 Proverbs 13:3 NKJV
6 Proverbs 10:19 NKJV
7 Proverbs 18:13 NKJV
8 Leviticus 20:9 NKJV
9 Proverbs 12:22 NKJV
10 Matthew 12:36 NKJV
11 Matthew 12:37 NKJV
12 James 3:6
13 Psalm 119:11
14 Jeremiah 17:9 NKJV
15 Matthew 6:19-20 NKJV
16 Matthew 6:24 NKJV
17 Proverbs 13:22 NKJV
18 2 Corinthians 12:14 NKJV
19 Matthew 12:33
20 Matthew 7:18
21 Galatians 5:22-23
22 Psalm 51:10 NKJV
23 Strong's 1254 (Hebrew)
24 1 Peter 3:15
25 2 Chronicles 30:12
26 Ephesians 5:19
27 Proverbs 4:23
28 Proverbs 23:7
29 1 Samuel 16:7
30 Psalm 95:8
31 Proverbs 25:20
32 Psalm 119:10

Chapter 13

1 Philippians 4:13 NKJV
2 Isaiah 40:31 NKJV
3 Galatians 6:9
4 Numbers 23:19
5 Romans 8:29
6 Strong's 38 (Greek)
7 2 Corinthians 6:17 NKJV
8 Romans 8:9
9 1 Peter 2:11 NKJV
10 1 Peter 5:9
11 1 Peter 5:10 NKJV
12 Hebrews 12:1
13 Mark 4:13, Luke 8:10
14 Isaiah 64:6
15 Romans 13:14
16 2 Corinthians 5:17
17 Ephesians 6:10-17
18 Romans 13:12
19 Isaiah 61:3
20 Philippians 3:10
21 Matthew 28:19-20, Mark 16:15
22 Strong's 1248 (Greek)
23 Ephesians 6:20
24 Matthew 10:8

Chapter 14

1. Acts 11:26
2. Acts 9:2
3. John 14:6
4. James 2:19 NKJV
5. John 11:47-53
6. Matthew 12:34
7. Matthew 23:27
8. Luke 4:10-11, Psalm 91:11-12
9. Luke 9:23
10. I Corinthians 15:3
11. Hebrews 9:27 NKJV
12. Matthew 25:34 NKJV
13. Matthew 25:41 NKJV
14. Romans 3:23
15. Romans 6:23
16. John 3:16
17. 2 Corinthians 5:21
18. Isaiah 52:14 NKJV
19. John 18:12
20. John 18:22
21. Matthew 27:29
22. Luke 18:32
23. Matthew 27:19-26
24. Matthew 27:29
25. Matthew 27:30
26. Matthew 27:33
27. Matthew 27:35
28. Matthew 27:45,51
29. Matthew 26:42
30. Romans 10:13 NKJV
31. Romans 10:14 NKJV
32. Romans 10:9 NKJV
33. John 3:3
34. John 3:4 NKJV
35. 2 Corinthians 5:17
36. Acts 4:12
37. John 14:6

Chapter 15

1. Collier's Encyclopedia Vol. 4, pg. 158
2. Collier's Encyclopedia Vol. 4, pg. 158-159
3. 1 Peter 1:19
4. Acts 2:4
5. John 3:3
6. John 10:4
7. Revelation 21:27
8. Philippians 3:20
9. Strong's 1347 (Greek)
10. Strong's 1344 (Greek)
11. Romans 5:17
12. Matthew 16:26 NKJV
13. Romans 13:11-14 NKJV
14. Ephesians 4:24
15. 1 Peter 2:9
16. Jude 3
17. 1 Corinthians 6:11
18. Galatians 3:13
19. Ephesians 1:6
20. Psalm 5:12
21. Revelation 19:8
22. Ephesians 1:1, Philippians 1:1, Colossians 1:2
23. Romans 8:29
24. Isaiah 46:10
25. Philippians 3:9
26. Revelation 19:16
27. Psalm 19:1
28. Revelation 21:18
29. Revelation 21:19
30. Revelation 21:21
31. John 14:2-3
32. Revelation 21:4
33. Hebrews 9:16-17
34. Ephesians 1:11, 1 Peter 1:4

Chapter 16

1   Jeremiah 16:19
2   Psalm 103:3
3   1 Samuel 17:47
4   Romans 10:17 NKJV
5   Hebrews 4:12 ESV
6   Acts 20:31
7   James 1:5
8   Psalm 73:24
9   2 Timothy 3:16
10   Romans 15:13
11   Psalm 107:20
12   2 Timothy 3:16
13   Romans 8:31, Mark 10:27
14   Mathew 6:7
15   Genesis 3:8
16   1 Thessalonians 5:16-18
17   Matthew 26:40
18   Daniel 10:10-13
19   Matthew 26:39
20   1 Peter 3:20-21
21   1 Corinthians 10:2
22   Leviticus 8:6
23   Exodus 19:10-14
24   Acts 2:38
25   Mark 16:16
26   Matthew 28:19 NKJV
27   Strong's 907 (Greek)
28   Romans 6:4
29   Acts 2:45
30   Ephesians 5:27
31   Strong's 2842 (Greek)
32   Luke 10:1
33   Luke 23:26
34   Proverbs 21:2
35   Strong's 3144 (Greek)
36   3 John 3
37   2 Timothy 1:8
38   Mark 16:15
39   2 Corinthians 3:2
40   1 Peter 3:15
41   John 1:12
42   1 Corinthians 3:7-8
43   Luke 6:22-23 NKJV
44   Matthew 10:32-33
45   Matthew 19:26
46   Philippians 4:13

Chapter 17

1   Acts 2:4
2   John 3:3
3   2 Corinthians 5:17
4   Mark 10:28
5   Webster's II New College Dictionary
6   Ephesians 4:27
7   Acts 1:8
8   2 Timothy 4:7

Epilogue

1   John 12:50
2   Hebrews 12:2
3   John 14:12

CPSIA information can be obtained
at www.ICGtesting.com
Printed in the USA
LVHW040819201222
735579LV00005BA/217